THE REAL ESTATE
INVESTING
MANUAL

How Trends Make You
A Smarter Investor

Gabrielle Dahms

May *The Real Estate Investing Manual* guide you toward the path that is right for you. Equipped with the book's information, your interest and actions in real estate investing are bound to produce results. Please go to www.realestatemanuals.com review *A Real Estate Investing Manual* and claim your bonus gift.

DEDICATION

To all clients, colleagues, and friends who teach and
support me every day.

Thank you!

Table of Contents

WHY THIS BOOK?

I am a realtor (TM). I have represented sellers and buyers of residential real estate. After several years in real estate sales, I ventured into real estate investing. The overlap between real estate sales and real estate investing is similar in some respects. But real estate investment can be distinct from real estate sales. It can be a different world. In a time where permanent jobs with benefits are waning, real estate investing appeals to many people. Some are in search of security, others want to become rich. All want to better themselves.

In addition, communities we live in can benefit from real estate investing. The ideal result is a fairer, more caring, and open society. Investors can succeed and make a positive difference where they own by delivering on demand for societal trends combined with local markets. As real estate investors, we must examine our underlying societal values and personal desires.

And women will play a much bigger role in real estate investing and in improving their communities. The real estate sales business has no gender requirements and showcases several successful women.

But in commercial real estate and in real estate investing women are not yet well-represented. It is time to change this.

The book aims to inspire as many women and men as possible to become successful real estate investors. That is you. Better yet, I would love for you to soar to financial independence and to continue to improve your communities.

Happy reading & investing!

INTRODUCTION

So, you want to become a real estate investor? Perhaps you already are one. Millions dream of being real estate investors. They imagine riches. They want to travel, drive a Jaguar, live in a beautiful home. Or they want to leave a legacy to their children, bask in success, or help their family, or choose to work or pursue their interests and hobbies. To some, freedom is the driving force, to others stability. Countless books, podcasts, and seminar gurus feed such desires. So why another book?

The book discusses the nut and bolts of real estate investing. It helps to relate real estate investing to the world around you. It delves into real estate trends and their defining sub-trends. It then segues into more nuanced perspectives to international, national, regional, state, and local levels.

The larger picture rests on the fundamentals. In turn, proficient, savvy investors understand the fundamentals. Then they apply them to the problems and the opportunities that arise.

We paint our canvas with designs that work and that solve problems. The problems may be small or large. They may be our own or those of others. Either way, landlords, wholesalers, rehabbers, buy-and-hold investors, or developers solve problems. They use such tools as other people's money, leverage, and negotiation. Yet everything they do starts with a specific mindset which the book explores.

We also take a holistic approach to personal and business finance. Several strategies serve as a powerful vehicle for economic growth. Yet there can be a fine line between solid strategies and speculation. We will dissect what makes one real estate investment sound and another a gamble. And we will look at ways to protect ourselves and our investments.

We want to move from dream to reality. When a child learns to walk, he takes one step after the other. He wobbles. He falls. Many real estate investors have similar learning curves. The book's chapters lay out the practical information for the beginner or the veteran investor. It helps you create, test and carry out your real estate investing blueprint. The blueprint encompasses mindset, style, building and maintaining systems, networks, teams, financial knowledge, time, and motivation.

The chapters' content helps design your investment blueprint. The blueprint is the foundation for real estate investing. Once we have it, we still need to decide and act. The decisions we make and the actions we take create our results. Success depends on us. Guarantees for success do not exist.

We must be honest about where we are and where we want to be. As we aim to bridge the gap between the two, our approach, mindset, and demeanor shift. Ideally, we transition from a consumer mentality to becoming an owner and investor.

The question of how to survive real estate market cycles remains ever present. How to protect ourselves from downsides is just as important as owning a home or any other real estate asset. A simple, executable strategy addresses this.

The rules of the game serve well to help design the plan. Real estate at any level involves large sums of money, and that money may not be our own. When we buy a home or an investment property, we make significant financial decisions in our lives. We are in control of the decisions we make. Yet, how we arrive at them depends on our personality and whether we follow the crowd.

In my real estate career, I have listened to many casual real estate conversations and tips. I have also met people who followed the lure, then maybe googled the topic and began there. What I present in this book stays away from water cooler or cocktail party conversations, which may be fine to get ideas but then prove inadequate. As in the stock market, real estate creates whisperers.

What we need is quality information because what we do not know can hurt us. Once we have the information, we must investigate it. Only then can we act. It is, of course, possible to get lucky on a hunch or a tip. But why gamble? The risk is too high.

Remember when the real estate markets were booming in 2005 and 2006? Many party attendees turned out to be self-styled investors gloating about their real estate ability and how much money they made. People also got real estate licenses to cash in on the boom. Others joined at the height of the market, putting their money and themselves at risk. The talking ceased once the markets crashed, and many people lost their proverbial shirts. A dismaying picture.

Then, many people offered stunning amounts over the asking price in San Francisco. Unfortunately, many of them took out loans that could not survive a major correction. Only buyers who had the requisite cash to cover the difference could withstand a downturn. Other owners didn't have to sell but could not cover the value difference. The value of the asset did not justify a 30 to 50% increase above asking prices in those years, but people bought, anyway. The fear of losing out created actual losses.

The conventional boom years' wisdom went: 'just get into the market.' It led many buyers to live hand to mouth. Many of them went into short sale situations. Some even lost their homes or investment properties to foreclosure. The necessary information was available, but either ignored or waved aside. High property values tempted owners to use their properties as banks. Some people believed they were leveraging their properties and bought a few more buildings. Who cared about analysis when riding the wave seemed easier? Money was flowing like wine. Why worry?

I tell you about the boom years' mentality because conventional wisdom limits intelligent decision-making. And in life, everything is about mindset. Real estate investing is no exception. Mindset and attitude are so important that almost every chapter touches on them.

Some questions to ask include: What does living a rich life mean to you? The freedom to do what you want? The freedom to travel? Do you want to give back? Or to serve? Think about it. What is it you want?

One final note about the structure of the book is that you can read the book from cover to cover or only read chapters that interest you. At the end of each chapter, a summary of the chapter's main points will help to spur your memory and add to your real estate investing foundation.

> *You've got to get to the stage in life where going for it is more important than winning or losing.*
> *– Arthur Asher*

CHAPTER 1

WHAT IS REAL ESTATE?

Let's begin with a quick overview of what real estate is. You may think of single-family homes or apartment buildings and so on. But it is land that underlies all real estate. Land is an immovable asset. We cannot make more of it. Real estate also refers to buildings on the land (real property) and sometimes to the natural resources the land holds. And the term real estate refers to its legal definition derived from English common law. In countries like the United States real estate falls under this legal system.

Many other countries in the world have different legal frameworks for real estate. The international real estate investor needs to know this. In some countries, real estate changes hands differently than in the United States. Finance practices are also different in different countries.

In Europe, for instance, loans to purchase real estate with are non-recourse loans. Non-recourse loans mean that only the property loaned on serves as collateral for the loan. In case of default, the bank cannot go after any other assets the borrower owns. In contrast, in the United States recourse loans are typical. The banks can go after the property and other assets owned by the borrower in case of defaults.

One exception to this is investing in real estate with a self-directed IRA. A borrower who takes out a loan for a property via her self-directed IRA can secure a non-recourse loan. Most investors who use self-directed IRAs pay cash, however.

Real estate has many classifications and sub-classifications. Those offer various avenues to invest in real estate. Every classification has pros and cons alongside specific evaluation criteria. Different classifications hold different appeal. Take the residential real estate classification which includes townhomes, condos, single-family homes, 1-4 multi-family buildings, cooperatives, TICs, mobile homes, and modular homes. Commercial real estate classifications include office buildings, warehouses, restaurants, hotels, 5+-unit multi-family and apartment buildings, retail spaces, parking lots, mobile home parks, and many others.

Residential and commercial real estate differ in important ways. Numbers and projections drive commercial real estate. Commercial real estate aims to create cash flow, then to maximize the cash flow and minimize any expenses. Commercial real estate transactions are large and require large sums of money. Their selection, due diligence, loan, transaction processes, and closing can be long and expensive.

Moreover, some people believe that residential real estate is more 'emotional' and commercial real estate is a 'give me the facts' business. But in residential and in commercial real estate, both approaches exist and often complement one another.

Commercial real estate comprises much larger projects, properties, and developments. Large sums of money change hands. The larger scale promises much larger dollar returns. Commercial real estate depends on good business practices and on running the investments as businesses.

Residential real estate's distinguishing feature is that buyers usually live in the property they buy. And for their own homes buyers' personal living preferences often are less numbers oriented. Commercial real estate, on the other hand, delivers a product to the market. The product then generates income.

About the Value of Land

The underlying land of any building, parking lot, commercial structure, mobile home park, storage facility etc. is the real estate. Structures (buildings) can appear and disappear while land cannot. The land provides much of the value in real estate. Land is also a finite resource.

Take San Francisco as an example: the actual City and County of San Francisco sit on a peninsula roughly seven miles by seven miles. Land and real estate values are at a premium here. The underlying value of any property depends on the value of land. The city's tax assessor employs a specific formula for determining the value of the land and the structure on it.

Although San Francisco was expensive even thirty years ago, it then possessed a different demographic. Over time, San Francisco evolved from a small town to an international city; from a blue-collar city to being home to venture capital and a tech haven; from a city that attracted eccentric artist types to a city closer to the mainstream.

The growth, appreciation, and desirability of San Francisco happened for many reasons. Today many high-paying jobs attract people to San Francisco, and the land and buildings have even higher values.

Besides land, labor is the number one factor driving real estate values. Increasing numbers of people must move to large cities to work. This global trend puts upward pressure on real estate. Although we live in the digital age and people could work remotely, few do.

Modern cities favor luxury owners and buyers. People with high incomes or net worth versus those who are mid-level professionals (teachers etc.), not to mention those who work in low-level jobs or who are unemployed. People in the mid-level, low-level, and unemployed categories must move to the suburbs or farther out. Then they commute into the nearest city to work unless they have inherited or owned a property in any city before the trend began.

The Art and Science of Real Estate

Most of us are familiar with the adage that real estate is not rocket science. It contains truth. Still, we have not yet mastered the pieces to understand, assess, and become proficient in real estate investing.

When investing in real estate, the right questions are invaluable. As we get answers, we understand and assess what we are looking at and whether we need additional information. Asking the right questions increases knowledge. The more informed, the better.

Beyond understanding the given property, we must know economic conditions and market environments, and existing finance options. Supply and demand, the competition, the trends, and other factors also help to make the right investment decisions. Our motivations and dreams contribute as well. As we drill into our why, we become aware of how risk-tolerant we are. We also learn about our management style, how we approach relationships, and why we chose real estate.

All leads us to the right investments for us. It is a lot to consider. We may be tempted to throw the proverbial dart. It's real estate after all. Somewhere in the more obscure recesses of our being, we believe that real estate is a safe and good way to make money and to thrive. Maybe someone else told us this. Therefore, the rationale continues, what's the risk?

Indeed, many of us buy or invest in real estate by throwing darts. And we aren't even aware of it until we take responsibility for our real estate decisions and how we made them. Until that happens we lack a baseline. Anything can happen.

Yes, some people made lots of money in real estate. Many of them just followed what others did - their friends, associates, family - because it appeared to be the right action. And many with that same mindset also lost everything via bankruptcies, short sales, or even foreclosures when the 'right thing' came crashing down. Still, others held on to properties but they often paid a steep price.

Ask qualified, experienced, trusted people the right questions and you will lay a solid foundation. Listen to the answers with an open mind. If you think you already know the answer even asking the right questions will not save you. Qualified, experienced, trusted people must answer all the questions referenced here at the minimum. If they shirk the questions and pressure you to buy or invest, run. When the person listens and helps you make better real estate decisions, the relationship is likely long-term. Never underestimate its value.

In that vein, please understand that you must pay this person whether you move forward with buying or investing. It is only right, plain and simple.

Clients who have question after question after question, often about issues and items that exceed any realtor's knowledge wave a big red flag. A potential client of mine did this on every single property we saw and ran pages of numbers and spreadsheets. She could not decide. This happens to many real estate professionals and real estate investors because they allow it.

I want to be clear here: some prospects become clients after years of just sitting in the real estate agent's database. This is fine. We all have life circumstances that affect us, events like losing a job, getting a divorce, taking care of an elderly parent and so forth. Motivation to own real estate also changes. But there is a fine line between someone who keeps thinking about owning property and a person ready to move forward.

But let's return to our topic. After we ask the right questions and evaluate the answers, our analysis of statistics and numbers begins. Comparables (comps) serve as a starting point. They never tell the whole story, but they signal and provide the general value background.

On par with the numbers and values stated in a stock company's Annual Report, real estate analyses have their own long list of statistics and projections. Some of these numbers, values, and assumptions are more important, some less. Even so, consider them in the context of the market. Ignore them at your own peril. Real estate is an art and a science in which experience, knowledge, and integrity play important roles. Without melding all components real estate buyers, sellers, and investors drift rudderless at sea.

What Cushions You When You Make a Mistake?

There are no guarantees in real estate investing. While that may sound harsh, many people have lost just as much money in real estate investing as they have made. How is that possible? Let's begin with real estate values, then move on to local, state, national, and international factors in real estate investor. Real estate functions in local, state, national, and international economic force fields. The actual real estate asset's value, therefore, depends on many factors. Even if a real estate investor is savvy, she or he is not immune to factors outside their control. Given this complex and somewhat unpredictable environment, mistakes happen, and things can go south in a hurry – and to the tune of millions of dollars at that.

Yes, there are people who claim they can predict the real estate markets. Practice caution when you meet them. Always think for yourself instead of following others' advice without vetting it.

Moreover, flexibility and a backup plan are prudent choices. We all hope and pray that we will be the investor who makes money. But to succeed, understanding the rules and having a plan go a long way.

A plan has immeasurable value because real estate investing has far-reaching consequences. It affects many people's lives, not just the investor's. For example, investors who raise capital for their visions and dreams, enroll other people who invest in them. That money many times stands for endless hours of toiling and for the dreams of those investors. Real estate investors, therefore, have fiduciary responsibilities just like licensed real estate professionals. These professionals, including you, hold other people's lives in their hands.

Functionary	Fiduciary
Low level	High level
Tells & Sells	Educates & Guides
Assumes little responsibility	Accepts high responsibility
Low Skill	High Skill
Delivers information	Advises & consults
Completes tasks	Owns the results
Replaceable	Irreplaceable
Tactical	Strategic
Follows rules & procedures	Uses judgment & intuition

[This table provides insight into vital differences between functionaries and fiduciaries. It is not a conclusive list. A true fiduciary puts his or her client's interest above all.]

If that sounds dire, realize that your success depends on other people's money, dreams and desires, labor, ideas, and so forth. Treat others well. Do not expose them to unnecessary risk. Communicate with them and use good risk mitigation practices.

Even then, failure can still happen. There, I have said the feared F–Word. Real estate investors are businessmen and businesswomen who must consider the possibility of it happening without flinching, without brushing over it. Failure in anything is a great teacher, so long as the person experiencing it possesses the mindset and the ability to rise from it. We'll return to this later in more detail.

Mistakes are inevitable. They happen. When they do, take responsibility. Assess what happened. Then improve yourself, your process, your network, your team, your way of doing business, and re-enter the field. In theory, this sounds easy enough, but it is much harder to put into practice. It takes incredible discipline and commitment.

Mitigating Risk

It may sound obvious that understanding market cycles helps investors. Market cycles continue always. Supply and demand drive markets. And factors like job creation, cost of living, inventory, interest rates, money supply, legislative changes and others affect supply and demand. In fact, any real estate investor will be in market cycles from start to finish. By the same token, over analyzing may produce adverse results.

The best way to mitigating risk includes excellent due diligence, which sounds easy but is difficult and sometimes intensive. A tried and true due diligence process is a great start. Many real estate investors and coaches send such a list as an enticement to do business with them. Why? Because the list serves as a starting point. You must be able to execute every checkpoint. Dig deeper than the list suggests. Once you learn how to do this, it will save you money and many headaches.

Further, have a plan, a strategy. With good strategy things progress better. The plan and strategy must include potential pitfalls and assess at least some risks before they ever happen. In the best-case scenario, they never happen but your strategy must address them. Things can arise that fall outside the plan. Still, as you think about potential risks, you increase your chance for getting appropriate responses. Plan for the downsides. When they occur, analyze them and learn from them. Your exit strategy is a component of mitigating risk.

Once your plan and strategy are in place, stick to it. Why is this important? It is easy to get distracted and venture off path by other, related ventures. It is a great temptation for real estate investors, even for those who have experience. A better action plan is to execute the initial plan and strategy, and to stay away from immaterial items.

Refine your plan as you go along; to tweak it so it is just right for you and works. Again, this may sound simple, yet inexperience can lead to the wrong refinements and tweaks.

A solid plan and strategy will also allow for integrity. You may wonder why integrity is such a big deal. The clearest answer is that real estate is a people business. The players know each other, often well. It may be fine to single-mindedly invest for the money. After a while, though, other aspects arise. Those include understanding your why and your motivation. It helps to ascertain others' motivation as well.

Most books never address realistic expectations or greed. The latter is prevalent and sometimes it causes real estate investors to lose good judgment, in the process treating others poorly. It is tempting to extract every penny without regard for anything else. It is subtle and almost imperceptible at times but not worth it. Ever.

Real estate investors also experience adversity. When adversity hits maintain a cool head, assess the situation and begin to problem-solve. Real estate investing requires resilience. When adversity hits, having the right people on your team can make all the difference. Beyond that, knowing when to quit has value.

Adversity carries lessons that propel the investor forward. Unforeseen consequences of adversity include personal, financial, and emotional consequences. In this context, resilience means doing the best (sometimes most courageous) thing possible for the circumstance. It also implies moving forward. Mental toughness is one definition for this but resilience is about the character of a person.

7 Real Estate Investing Rules

1. Buy for cash flow, not for appreciation

2. Be conservative.

3. Think long-term.

4. Have sufficient cash reserves.

5. Enroll others in your vision.

6. Treat others with respect.

7. Do all your homework.

The Desire to Create Wealth

Most of us want to be wealthy. The common understanding of wealth is financial and material wealth, and real estate is a wonderful vehicle to create it. Real Estate offers many asset classes and a variety of ways to generate income and appreciation.

Real estate is a hybrid asset class with land as its underlying asset. Land is an illiquid asset, but the asset class can have liquidity depending on what is being done with it. For instance, if raw land sits fallow, the investor pays annual property taxes on it but the land generates no income. Then again, the investor could asphalt the land and put it into service as a parking lot. Now it generates income. These two approaches encompass appreciation versus cash flow.

Remember that true wealth is more than financial wealth. It refers to a holistic approach that considers the whole person. We all create the wealth we experience in our lives. A person's wealth consists of physical, intellectual, spiritual, relational and financial wealth. Real estate creates financial wealth and becomes a part of true wealth.

But how are true wealth and being a true investor related? If an investor's sole aim is to make money, other areas in his life can fall apart. The carnage includes failed relationships, arrogance, losing it all, not knowing who one's friends are, and choosing money and profit over doing what is right. -Wealth of any kind requires humility, smarts, and understanding and appreciating the bigger picture.

Let's take a brief look at how wealth and the American Dream show up in the American psyche so that we can understand today's trends in our society and the impact they have on real estate investing even better.

The American Dream

Many years have elapsed since the Founding Fathers pronounced that every American, could attain prosperity through hard work. In the early Republic this applied to white males. The pull-yourself-up-from-the-bootstraps ideal continues to inform Americans to this day. Now, the American Dream is open to almost all Americans. The dream's ideal pervades their hearts and minds. It promises a better, happier life. Owning property, at least one's home, is part of the Dream.

The Merriam-Webster dictionary defines the American Dream like this:

'a happy way of living that is thought of by many Americans as something that can be achieved by anyone in the U.S. especially by working hard and becoming successful.'

The prototypical American Dream consists of a good job, a nice house, two children, and plenty of money. But does the American Dream remain viable? Can it still become a reality given the changes in American society? Reality and the Dream often present different worlds and life experiences.

In recent years several observers of today's American reality have written and spoken about how the American Dream is less attainable today. Demographics, such as gender, education level, income level, and cost-of-living play a big role in attaining it. The American Dream costs money.

While the pull-yourself-up-from-the-bootstraps mentality may still be possible, it takes a lot more ingenuity to attain it. We live in a different and diverse America in which urban centers hold most of the jobs and opportunities. Yet, urban centers also require more money and income. Competition for anything from housing to education to jobs and job security is like standing in long lines for sparse goods every day in United States' cities.

On the American coasts, this pattern is more pronounced still. The possibility of owning a home, raising a family and educating one's children requires much more money here. In other US cities, like Detroit or Anchorage, the American Dream at first glance appears a viable option until realizing that job opportunities are less plentiful here. However, the correlation between the cost of living and the American Dream points to both the Midwest and the Southwest as regions where the Dream is still possible.

At the same time, many Americans can no longer live the American Dream. Economic growth patterns in the United States differ from they were in the 1940s and 1950s. Many well-paying jobs, manufacturing, and other jobs no longer exist. Communities, once thriving with good post-WW II economies, have become like ghost towns. Many younger Americans, those born from 1980 on, must leave their communities to seek their fortunes in the cities. Alongside the economic changes, inequality in America has risen and many opportunities exist for a few Americans only. The promise of a better, richer, fuller life has diminished from at least the 1950s on and that the American Dream is unattainable by an ever-growing number of Americans.

In a recent San Francisco Chronicle article by columnist Nick Hoppe, the following almost humorous imaginary dialogue appeared:[1]

Yes, there will be homes for sale. The question is where you will have to live to afford one.

I only have one grandchild, and she can't talk yet (or do much of anything), but if I had a couple in the vicinity of 12 years old, I expect we'd have the following conversation:

Little Jimmy: Grandpa, explain to us again why we'll never own our own home.

Me: That's not true, Little Jimmy. You can own your own home someday. You'll just have to move far, far away.

Little Susie (starting to cry): But I don't want to leave my friends and family.

Me (patting her little head): Don't be a crybaby, Little Susie. You might like Reno. Or Detroit. Or North Dakota.

Little Jimmy: I don't want to move, either. I want to stay in the Bay Area.

---

[1] Reprinted with the permission of the author.
https://www.sfchronicle.com/news/article/Dreaming-the-dream-of-home-ownership-12763192.php

Me: You're dreaming, kid. You also want to be a fireman. Get a grip. You'll never be able to afford a home around here.

Little Susie (drying her tears): Grandpa, tell us again about when you bought your first home. Did it really cost only $9,000?

I will sigh, knowing it will be hard for them to hear these stories, just like it was when I told my children. But it will also fascinate them because it is so surrealistic.

Me: It was a long, long time ago, in the late 1970s. Your grandmother and I were in our early 20s, and we found a one-bedroom, one-bath house on 41st and Shafter in Oakland. And I know it hurts your little ears to hear it, but we paid $9,000 for the whole house.

Little Susie: Mommy's car cost more than that!

Little Jimmy (sensing an opportunity): What would it sell for now?

Me: Probably more than you could ever afford. We sold it a year later for more than we paid and bought something else. Then we sold that and bought something else. It was loads of fun. Too bad you kids won't ever have that opportunity.

Little Jimmy (pouting): It's not fair. I want to buy a house someday.

Me: Too late, kiddo. But if it makes you feel any better, it's too late for your Mommy and Daddy, too.

Little Susie: That doesn't make me feel any better. And I don't understand — they make lots of money.

Me: Not enough for around here. Unless your Daddy or Mommy starts a successful tech company or wins big in the lottery, you're all destined to pay exorbitant rents forever if you want to stay in the Bay Area. Owning a home is out of the question.

Little Jimmy (showing incredible financial acumen for a 12-year-old): If interest rates rise and the new tax law limits property tax write-offs to $10,000, won't that lower real estate values?

Me: Good question, Little Jimmy. Maybe a little. But you still won't be able to afford Bay Area prices. When we bought our first house, interest rates were close to 10 percent. It didn't stop prices from going up in the Bay Area.

Little Susie: Grandpa, you're supposed to encourage us in life. Why are you being such a jerk?

Me: Sorry, Little Susie. I'm just telling it like it is. Your generation got royally screwed.

Little Susie: GRANDPA!

Me: Excuse my bluntness, but it's true. My generation could buy a house for peanuts, make no improvements and sell it for a ridiculous profit years later. Your generation is stuck using all your income to pay thousands per month in rent for a one-bedroom apartment. But no one said life is fair.

Little Jimmy (pulling out his laptop and typing away): Check it out, Little Susie. Here's a three-bedroom house for sale for $45,000. And here's another one for $69,000. I can still be a fireman and own my own house after all.

Little Susie (eagerly looking over Little Jimmy's shoulder): This is so exciting. There's another one for $54,995. Grandpa is right as usual. Mommy and Daddy can buy any of these houses right now. All we have to do is move to Detroit.

Me (beaming): I'm proud of both of you. The American dream of homeownership is alive and well. Just not around here.

Little Jimmy: Grandpa, if we buy this Detroit house for $45,000, will it be worth a lot more in a few years, just like your houses were?

Me (hugging them both): Maybe, Little Jimmy. Maybe. But don't forget my sweet munchkins — you'll be in Detroit.

The American Dream & Real Estate Investors

The American Dream paints a larger canvas, a backdrop, for real estate investors. Individual investors may in fact dream the Dream themselves, including in the scenario in which they perceive that they can only attain the Dream as real estate investors. Many smaller investors belong to this category.

Images of the early American republic spring to mind: settlers claiming their land and homestead. Real estate still holds allure even if times have changed. Searching for great real estate deals is like panning for gold. The rush on real estate almost suggests that it is happening. And just like during the Gold Rush, the world of real estate can be rugged and rough, its promise so appealing as to attract speculators versus investors. Real estate and real estate investing has enriched many men and wiped out many others.

Put differently, the potential for riches does not equal the American Dream. The perhaps more upbeat truth for today's real estate investors is that understanding the trends, the changing American landscape discussed above and throughout this book offers some stunning opportunities. One example is that many Millennials cannot afford their own homes but they need a place to live. Multi-family and apartment building real estate investors stand to benefit. So long as the investor investigates, knows, and delivers what Millennials need and desire. Another opportunity might be to offer lease-options to Millennials, providing an avenue to own their own homes down the line. Other variations on the theme are limitless, provided sound business principles apply. They assist real estate investors in serving Americans.

When to buy and invest in real estate?

Now, you may wonder whether there is a right or a wrong time to buy real estate. People often ask me questions like 'what do you think of the market?' and 'where do you think it's headed?' What they really want to know is whether it is the right time to buy, sell, or invest in real estate.

In my experience, the answer to the question is there is a right time to buy, sell or invest in real estate is 'when you are ready.' I mean the time when you know what you want and can afford and act. Every person has a different timeline.

In real estate opportunity abounds for those with discernment of what to seek and those conscious of their tolerance levels, etc. That is true in all market environments. While knowing the market environment helps to decide, buying, selling, or investing in real estate are personal decisions. The person's readiness is more important than the market environment. In addition, opportunities exist in all market environments.

And now let's take a closer look at the trends and their effects on real estate ownership and investing.

CHAPTER 2

THE TRENDS & REAL ESTATE INVESTING

Go Global

It comes as no surprise that real estate investing has global appeal. Land and property exist everywhere. But global real estate as a business is more complex. Urbanization, job, and economic growth drive the international real estate markets - just as they do in the United States. But different models, rules, regulations, and laws lay the foundations of international real estate.

As this book goes to publication, large amounts of capital are flowing into the international real estate markets, even as markets feel the effects of rising interest rates, for example. More capital equals more competition and more risk. Innovation and technology differentiate international real estate investors.

As always, understanding local markets is tantamount. But in international real estate investing we also must understand how markets interact. The flow of money influences the international real estate business. And we must know what challenges present themselves when owning and operating internationally. In international real estate assets, profits materialize by maximizing property performance.

If real estate investing in the United States is about identifying a market niche that has problems and solving them, this applies to international real estate as well. And trends we discussed before also apply internationally, especially the affordable and senior housing trends. Other possibilities for the international real estate investor revolve around resort development, housing for students, and business/office center development.

International real estate investing is not for the faint of heart. It requires know-how, adaptability, increased and efficient use of technology, and sophistication. For newer real estate investors these required elements point to a steep learning curve that demands money, time, and effort. For seasoned real estate investor pros international real estate investing offers excitement and profits. Among the many factors to consider are increasing capital flow to the international real estate markets, low inventory, varied monetary policy, and possible market demand shifts.

Beginning real estate investors might consider investing in REITs with international holdings or in exploring synergistic partnerships with seasoned real estate investing professionals.

International real estate investing offers opportunities. Overall Cap rates stay stable, but investors must know the market cycles for the countries and cities where they own. Market cycles make a huge difference. For instance, now Brisbane, Australia is in an accelerating cycle, while Tokyo is a peaking cycle and Seoul, Korea is in a bottoming cycle.[2]

Investing internationally is one thing. Another is that even if investing in real estate locally, the effect of the global market is palpable. The United States market responds to capital flow and interactions with investors from other countries. Those from the United States who invest in other countries also have an effect. At the least, being aware of the world of international real estate is prudent.

Paying with Cryptocurrency

Crypto currency like Bitcoin, Monero, Ethereum, Dash, and others are blockchain technology. Cryptocurrency aims to create more secure monetary transactions. In a world where hackers thrive, and inventive scams abound that is a welcome sentiment. Almost all legitimate service providers facilitating large financial transactions, like title companies, regularly and consistently caution consumers about the latest scams.

Crypto currency works through a linear series of blocks of code which then create a record of each transaction. What underlies the unique access codes is blockchain technology. Those access codes then become available for use almost worldwide. Because this streamlines the transaction process, third parties like title companies and banks,

---

[2] Data from Morgan Stanley's Global Real Estate Analysis for 2018

are no longer needed. Cryptocurrencies help making and receiving payments anywhere, any time.

Anyone who has ever transacted real estate where money came from other countries, may sigh in relief. Cryptocurrency appears to have much less red tape although governments have yet to regulate it. Regulation is apt to happen.

Overall, cryptocurrency offers advantages in real estate transactions. It does not include sensitive customer data in transactions. Users can encrypt and protect their funds. They can also choose associated fees these fees are not tied to transfer amounts. So far, manipulation of cryptocurrency is not possible and has not happened.

Real estate transactions and cryptocurrencies offer the perfect match. In theory anyway. In markets like San Francisco and New York luxury homes may accept Bitcoin but most buyers, sellers, and real estate professionals do not yet understand the technology.

Property down payments with Bitcoin are becoming hip among a crowd more familiar with digital money. Per Bloomberg Technology, 71% of Bitcoin owners are males between the ages of 18 and 34 years old. These young men appear to distrust the government and, to a degree, the markets. Since the currency is not yet regulated and has wild value swings, those most attracted to it are the technology-savvy and speculator types.

And even though digital currency has value, a third-party fiduciary who specializes in cryptocurrency serves to convert it into good old greenbacks. Yes, the conversion is from digital currency to hard cold cash because that is what sellers want. On average, this costs 10% of the transaction value.

The International Blockchain Real Estate Association (a trade organization founded in 2013) highlights the reasons cryptocurrencies are great in real estate transactions. Here is what the IBREA homepage states: it can reduce costs, stamp out fraud, speed up transactions, increase financial privacy, internationalize markets, and make real estate a liquid asset.

Sounds amazing?

Not so fast. Cryptocurrencies have challenges. The technology can bolster cybersecurity but it cannot by itself prevent cyber fraud. Another issue is volatility of the currencies. And competitors exist as well. Perhaps most importantly, the public and the consumer do not yet understand cryptocurrency. Consumers have yet to accept cryptocurrency as a practical way to pay and/or receive large sums of money in real estate transactions.

Interestingly, cryptocurrency has found more application in the real estate rental market. For example, ManageGo, a New York City property management company, accepts virtual currency to appeal to techie renters.

The trend to move to cryptocurrency to consummate real estate transactions is important to note. That is because the underlying issues, viewed through the lens of cryptocurrency advantages, are real and demand solutions. Real estate investor at least ought to follow this trend to assess how the underlying issues affect them in their real estate investing business.

Blockchain Technology

Blockchain technology underlies cryptocurrency and allows consumers to create contracts through an 'if, then' process. It has the potential of replacing realtors and lawyers in real estate transactions. Although real estate transactions are complex and the transaction process can change, blockchain technology could well appeal to many consumers. Many consumers want to save commissions and do not understand what real estate professionals do. Blockchain technology also appeals to do-it-yourself types.

With blockchain technology in place, imagine the consumer just calling the first real estate professional that comes to mind, asking: what would you do in this situation, circumstance etc.? This free advice syndrome already exists in the industry, like what doctors and lawyers get when they state their professions. Blockchain technology encourages consumers to take this to the next level: implying and believing they can do the transaction themselves yet calling the professionals for free advice.

Okay, perhaps that is too dim a view. I believe blockchain technology's positives lie in the transparency the technology can create in real estate. And transparency in anything from title searches, transaction management, to escrows is a good thing. The possibility of diminished fees and more expediency exists as well.

We are on the road to digital real estate transactions but they are not yet fully digital. Still, imagine that the consumer goes online, sees photos, virtual tours and so on, then purchases the property sight unseen. Some people are already doing this. When almost everybody buys real estate virtually only, then blockchain plays a much bigger role.

Blockchain technology promises to have a big impact, directly or indirectly, on how real estate data gets shared. The Multiple Listing Service (MLS) is proprietary and local. Although companies like Realtor.com, Zillow, and Trulia have leveraged the MLS, the data they present is often out of date. Consumers want access to real data without contact with a real estate professional. Blockchain technology could make the consumer's wish a reality unless Multiple Listing Services figure out a way to do this without being cut out as middlemen.

Recently, many Multiple Listing Services have begun conversations about the move to a national database, something consumers have demanded for a long time. Such conversations will gain traction as blockchain technology threatens proprietary services (the MLS). Note that blockchain technology lends itself to more linear processes but that listing property and connecting buyers and sellers may be bigger challenges. MLS' across the country are aware of this.

Blockchain technology builds on if-then clauses which self-execute. For real estate, this could mean that smart contracts are the way of the future. Even if smart contracts are a way off, the more immediate application of Blockchain technology lies in its potential to automate compliance. This is huge as anyone who has ever been a real estate professional will attest; it integrates complex regulatory and legal requirements.

Areas in which blockchain technology could play a bigger role is international real estate and commercial real estate by expediting due diligence, transactions, and cash flow efficiencies. In case you are interested in applying blockchain technology in the sphere of international real estate, the International Blockchain Real Estate Association may be your thing. The association has existed since 2013, and yes, the association accepts Bitcoin as payment.

Green Homes

The trend toward green homes to save resources is underway. Efficient management of resources occupies more homeowners today. Green living, including green homes, home automation, and green landscaping among others can pay huge dividends and do good for the environment. The choices we make have huge impacts on our quality of life. Traditional home building contains high chemical loads which leak into the land. The materials also outgas into the home itself. Green homes minimize toxic loads.

Energy-efficient homes and home building have been around for decades, albeit mostly on the fringes until recently.

Growing populations tax the earth's resources. We consume enormous amounts of resources to urbanize and build. Our consumption razes forests. New problems arise. Deforestation causes sustainability issues, increased waste, water management problems, air quality, land use and conservation issues. As real estate investors, we can make a big difference in building more sustainably–with a conservationist attitude.

Consumers now demand good conservation practices and more sustainable ways to build efficient homes. Good environmental deeds create consumer appeal. Consumers want to save, and investors stand to make money.

By replacing prevailing home building practices, greener building occurs. Until now, conventional building practices were more efficient and cost-effective. But in the last two decades, back-end costs of conventional home building have become plain. Green building trends' benefits warrant more attention now. As life gets more expensive, space comes at a premium, and more toxins assault us, green homes might well offer cost-effective alternatives. They have less environmental impact plus they offer energy savings besides comfort.

Green homes will evolve in the coming decades because they offer important solutions to housing more people and conserve natural resources. Property design of the future aims to achieve space efficiency, sustainability, and affordability. Green building extends from intelligent property placement and smart property design to using green materials for walls and roofs. Wind and solar power, compostable toilets, water efficiency, drought-resistant sustainable landscaping, automated and efficient homes (smart homes) all contribute.

The old stigma that green building costs more is no longer true. Costs, as with traditional building, depend on individual tastes and choices. The choice is to build high-end and low-end properties in an environmentally friendly fashion. Builders can opt to incorporate one or two green elements or go green all the way. All traditional building materials, furnishings, and appliances have green alternatives. Green building materials are non-toxic, durable, non-polluting, locally produced and sourced, natural, renewable, and/or recycled sustainable building products.

Real estate investors will benefit from the green building trend as this trend offers various opportunities. Investors can build or improve properties that are green. This saves resources and even maintenance down the line. Green building also often offers a more efficient way to use space, increasing the real estate investor's bottom line. The investor may further test which demographic demands green building. Vision and imagination alongside solid planning and understanding the building site or the existing structure help investors to deliver. Green building is a *sky's the limit* opportunity for real estate investors.

Many books deal with the nitty-gritty of going green in real estate. We mention the trend so you are aware of it. Educate yourself more about green building before you jump on the bandwagon.

Technology

Technology is here to stay. It evolves every single day. In real estate the use of drones, digital technologies like DocuSign, transaction management systems, and blockchain are now commonplace. As consumers all of us experience the onslaught of the new, the innovative, the sometimes weird. In traditional real estate, automated first contacts between real estate customers or potential ones and real estate professionals are standard now. Automated computerized functions in effect free the real estate professionals' by providing customer service and lead generation. The goal is to engage the customer.

Just a short mention: the U.S. real estate industry is a behemoth. The industry's proprietary technologies, most notably the MLS, are now under pressure to adapt and to become more transparent. Consumers want to save money. Emerging technologies promise savings and ease and they put pressure on the industry.

The discussion about consumers having direct and limitless access to the local MLS is ongoing. Local MLS' have up-to-date information and contain certain information that is only available on the MLS. Sites which aggregate MLS listings, like Zillow, Trulia, Open Listings and Redfin do not show complete data. As a proprietary network, the MLS information is only available to paying members. For the moment, consumers have access to the local MLS via real estate agents only. And the National Association of Realtors aims to strengthen the access via agents only by allowing brokers not to have their listings show up on sites like Zillow.

Yet, exclusivity of local and regional MLS's remains at issue. The Center for Data Innovation published a study in November 2017 which argues that consumers are being harmed by the MLS. According to the study, the harm lies in having no direct access to MLS data. The study referred to Redfin which rebutted its theses. However, the study suggests potential anti-trust issues. A new real estate business model may have arrived: tech and real estate appear a perfect match. All this points to possibilities for innovation in the real estate industry.

Tech real estate solutions have their basis in presenting data in a mobile format with the idea to ease the purchase of the home. Too bad that the old proprietary model of real estate seems to be what the techies propound, albeit virtually.

Make no mistake, the most intelligent buying decision still stems from seeing the property. Tech companies have little interest in doing this work. They believe their apps suffice. But overall, the apps remove any service component, making property buying and selling a commodity.

Still, techies who promote their new visions of how to buy and sell real estate feel they are doing all the work. They sit behind computers and have little idea about property. The residential real estate business appeals to them because they see profits without doing the actual work.

That's fine if clients understand what they are paying for and what they can expect. All real estate app companies make a nice tidy profit unless they can undercut the market with venture capital funding in place. They do so by making a huge marketing splash - yes, presentation matters - without doing much of the work that traditional agents do.

What is great about this particular development is the reminder to real estate professionals to deliver amazing service and to educate clients about the professional's role.

By the same token, emerging digital technologies and other technological solutions are disrupting the current real estate industry model. Innovation is the name of the game. Venture-funded, technology start-ups continue to enter the space, attracted by high-profit potential. Several such companies have come and gone but new ones or re-invented ones continue to arrive. Information real estate agents traditionally had a monopoly on is now more widely available to real estate investors.

A realtor only makes money when the sales transaction completes. In contrast, tech companies are more like a separate MLS and charge access fees and monthly fees. They can do so because they hold a real estate license. But the license does not make them active, traditional realtors ™. In addition, tech companies charge referral fees because consumers still want a live person to guide them.

Given these developments, the real estate industry must adapt. Those who cannot adapt will exit the industry. For real estate investors, these developments encourage innovation. Investors benefit by understanding how traditional real estate works and how the field is changing. That is especially true if they are technologically adept.

New technologies constantly arrive, and older ones get overhauls. Easier access to vital information, to more streamlined and time- and money-saving systems, to the ability to connecting virtually first propel to success. Technology used well increases profit margins, saves time, increases productivity, and reduces costs. - Note that the 'old way' of doing real estate is still a valid, effective model for real estate investors. While technology is beautiful (when it works!), the right network is a huge advantage. The right network and traditional real estate work just fine.

The Agentless Transaction

Alongside the technology trend, the agentless transaction is making a comeback. Formerly For-Sale-By-Owner listings were the prototypical agentless transactions, although many FSBO eventually ended up traditional listings. Reasons they became traditional listings included that many FSBO sellers had no way to distinguish qualified buying prospects from penniless looky-loos. Sellers also carried enormous liability by having no representation. They often could not get the price they wanted for their properties. All those issues are multifaceted stories in themselves. FSBOs still exist, especially in less competitive markets, but now a new breed of agentless transactions is on the horizon.

Technology has advanced the agent-less transaction. Websites that offer agent-less services to sellers keep emerging. If the site is well-designed, it offers great listing pages, video, e-mail capabilities for the buying and selling parties, and offer forms. Less clear is whether the property gets market exposure to potential buyers. In other words, what kind of market exposure does the property get?

Savvy real estate professionals and real estate investors know this and scour those websites at regular intervals, then approach the sellers. Although many sellers on these sites resist real estate investors and real estate professionals, many of them talk with one or both, eventually. They may even end up selling to the investor or listing the property with an agent. For our purposes, just know finding a receptive and willing seller this way is time-consuming.

As a humorous aside, often attorney clients present the greatest challenges for real estate professionals. In the almost two decades in my real estate career, most – though not all – of my attorney clients are persnickety about standard real estate contracts. One of my clients literally read every single word in the contract, then highlighted all words offending to him, and requested to re-write the entire contract. Don't get me wrong. Reading the contract is good practice.

The challenge was that real estate attorneys wrote both the California and San Francisco-specific contracts. Further, special items can be amended and incorporated by specific written-in language, albeit without crossing out wording and lines in the contract!

Naturally, any contract can be re-written but It takes time and money to do so. Then, once the other party reads that contract confusion ensues. And the other party must engage their own legal counsel to figure it all out and respond appropriately.

Yep, re-writing a real estate contract is fine and dandy but watch the property or the interested buyer or seller go away in a hurry. The good news is that sophisticated attorney clients know this. Many of them work well with real estate professionals to get what they want.

But let's return to the trend of the agentless transaction, which is about many of the trends we already mentioned. A quick recap: many factors are shaping up right now (2018) that will define the role of realtors in tomorrow's world. Among them are:

1. Blockchain technology

2. Apps, websites, and programs to empower the consumer

3. A vanishing personal interaction.

4. A changing role for realtors ™.

5. A more educated and sophisticated consumer.

6. Discussions about the MLS becoming a public tool.

Many consumers already know the data. What they don't know is what else is important. Even if they do, how to evaluate the data eludes them. Consumers may even be great negotiators but realize that real estate negotiations are complex and time-consuming and so they seek advocacy.

The idea of agentless transactions encapsulates the paradox of real estate which is its simplicity and simultaneously its complexity. Many real estate start-ups aim to streamline transactions, to add transparency, and to enable online referral networks. Most real estate start-ups are well-intentioned. They understand that profits stem from connecting buyers and sellers to real estate agents.

While a few apps that want to reform the real estate industry by removing commissions, they have yet to gain traction. Tech applications mostly spin the traditional model for online use.

Arriving at agentless transactions takes more than websites, apps, and technological offerings in their current form. For one, agent-less transactions are fine when all goes well in the transaction. When there are issues, such as title issues, financing problems, problematic inspection reports, or personality clashes arise, technology presents no workable solutions. So far, technological advances emphasize real estate marketing and facilitation. They lack thorough analysis, knowledge, experience, guidance, and negotiation.

Although technology cannot replace a true fiduciary, it speeds up transactions. Still, agents remain as important as true fiduciaries. The agent of the future will be a counselor and an educator, a trusted advisor versus a transactional figure. Only agents that understand their clients, their concerns, their needs and their questions will stay in business, at least in the long-term.

Co-Living and Communal Living

Another trend in real estate regards community. Anything from collaborative workspace designs, to senior housing and to co-housing belongs to this trend. Before you point out the 1960s and 70s, consider that today communal living almost exclusively stems from housing shortages. The impetus for today's trend differs greatly from that of the 1960s and 70s, which had philosophical underpinnings to create a better, freer world. Today's trend, in contrast, is about affordability.

Interestingly, the trend is strongest in cities like New York, Washington, and San Francisco where rents are sky high. Millennials, in particular, consider co-living. Generally, co-living properties come furnished, share the kitchen and bathroom space, and offer amenities to renters. Professional management exists in most co-living properties. The properties are similar to regular rentals. They have lease agreements in place, but the rents are more affordable than those of apartments in similar locations.

Co-living properties offer investors a niche market, but investors must know the local rental market, its rules and regulations, zoning, and housing codes backward and forward. Real estate investors can either develop such properties themselves or collaborate with real estate developers. Other options include constructing new properties or development of properties with expansion potential.

If the co-living trend appeals to you, locate the right market and line up financing. The financing might be a bigger hurdle than many other pieces we mentioned because lenders still are relatively unfamiliar with co-living properties. Finding a lender or even an investor (unless you have the money yourself) can be a tough sled. Aside from using your own funds, local banks may be a great alternative to get co-living projects funded. As always, have a business plan in hand when approaching local banks once you have developed the relationship.

The trend toward community-focused real estate developments fuels the future because almost all people want to know their neighbors. Those reared on technology may connect via texts and social media and have huge networks. But the connections and networks are a bit deceptive. That's because technology also contributes to living in more isolation than earlier generations experienced. Properties that come alongside a community, one the real estate investor or developer curates, have an appeal for this reason.

Co-living start-ups like The Collective and WeLive entice millennials. In commercial real estate, co-working spaces keep popping up in many cities, large and small, around the world. That means more money has been flowing into this trend. Opportunities for real estate investors abound. The trends center on building communities, and on bringing diversity and good quality of life together.

Investment in communal living communities demands vision, the ability to find the correct markets and locations, careful execution, and excellent property management. Sounds like a tall order, right? Many real estate investors will not touch this niche. For real estate investors who like a challenge, the co-living niche could be ideal though.

Further, community land trusts and co-housing aim to create neighborhoods within buildings or developments and to alleviate the loneliness many people experience in the modern world. For example, many Baby Boomer women never married and many Baby Boomer one-time couples now live apart or are divorced or widowed. Many live alone and often feel isolated. Co-housing communities exert a strong draw on these Boomers. Many Boomers are in much better health than their parents were at their age. They lead active lives, and they want independence. Co-housing can offer this.

Senior Housing

Senior housing and senior communities present yet another aspect of this trend. Many seniors live alone, some are downsizing. For various reasons, seniors move into either a senior community or into senior housing because they have special needs or seek certain comfort levels. This group of seniors can afford to move into communities they like.

The Baby Boomers are a huge demographic for 55+ housing and eventually senior housing. Although Boomer retirement has begun, a wave of Boomers will retire in another ten years, offering long-term opportunities for senior housing development. Boomers are unlikely to sit in rocking chairs to wait out their final years. One obvious opportunity for real estate investors is to develop or transform nursing homes into assisted living facilities. But senior living today is not what it once was. Today it requires excellent design, dining options, even entertainment connection to the world via the latest technologies.

An important consideration for investors in this market niche focuses on good operating companies. Assisted living investments depend on good operating companies. Unfortunately, a dearth of good operating companies existed until recently. However, more are likely to start up going forward, just in time for real estate investors to take part in this lucrative niche.

Seniors both rent and own properties but properties with specific requirements. Boundless opportunities exist for investors. The trend toward community ignites the investor's imagination. The ability to contribute to the fabric, development, and evolution of towns, cities, counties, states, countries and the world excite. And this happens as a by-product to making real estate investing an undertaking which fosters community.

The Gig Economy

Note the Gig Economy's impact on real estate investing. The Gig Economy refers to an economic environment in which many workers earn their living with a mosaic of temporary, short-term engagements. Over 40% of American workers work gigs, a number that will swell. The Gig Economy suggests a different modern-day American economy than the one a mere two decades earlier.

In the not so recent past gigs referred to job engagements for artists and musicians and defined 'no regular employment.' Companies like Uber, Lyft, Airbnb, TaskRabbit and many others changed how people work in today's America. Instead of changing places of employment as employees, growing numbers of Americans are independent contractors and freelancers, also known as Gig Workers.

Although many Gig Workers have the freedom to balance their lives with their work, job security, and benefits, elude these workers. Without a gig, the person generates no income. The gig produces income. It also exposes the Gigger to the risks and liabilities of the business, pays the operating expenses and also a percentage to the platform that got them the gig. Their choice to work when they want means a state of flux.

A report published by Intuit in 2010 predicted that by 2020, a year that is fast approaching, 40% of American workers would be part of the Gig Economy.[3] The number is close to the findings of the Edelman Intelligence study on freelance work from 2017. The 27-page Intuit report presents the Gig Economy glowingly and ends with the belief that big and small firms increasingly rely on each other's capabilities to better compete in the global marketplace.

Technology and social networks fuel the Gig economy, an online economy. But while many Gig Workers may start out as such, they then aim to become employees.

The Gig Economy has effects on real estate, specifically on populations in the market to own homes. Many Gig Workers cannot qualify for mortgages because the Gig Economy offers little stability or regular fixed income. Instead, Gig Worker's incomes can vary, shift and change. Many end up just making ends meet. That makes sense once we know that hourly compensation in this economy ranges between $11 and $28 on average. On those wages, Gig Workers then must pay for their own benefits and taxes.

Whether you love or hate the Gig Economy, it is here to stay. The trend is global. Real estate investors are smart to recognize this trend. While many Gig Workers may never afford or qualify for purchasing a home, at least not the traditional way, all of them need a place to live. Investors who note this trend could do very well in multi-family property or mobile home park investing.

---

[3] http://http-download.intuit.com/http.intuit/CMO/intuit/futureofsmallbusiness/intuit_2020_report.pdf

CHAPTER 3

DO THE MATH

Answers to questions and numbers' analysis set great deals apart from mediocre and poor ones. Knowledge and Numbers provide keys to residential or commercial real estate. However, the complexity of transactions differs for residential versus commercial real estate. It takes more time and more money to put together an in-depth analysis of commercial properties than for residential properties.

In-depth analysis is key in securing financing. In addition, make sure you understand what types and classes of property a lender will lend on. The lender's specific requirements are just as important. Complete the homework about the lender, then move on to the in-depth analysis, the baseline for the transaction.

When investing in other states:

1. Understand applicable real estate laws & practices in the state your investment is in.

2. Have a support team and vet them.

3. Consider tax rates.

4. Formulate an overall strategy.

5. Look at good deals only.

   Note that numbers and $$$ (price tags) may sound low compared to those in high property value states but may not represent a deal.

6. Observe the market dynamics where you are investing.

7. Develop an exit strategy

Steps to Success

- Run your own numbers for the property.

- Learn about the neighborhoods.

- Study the markets.

- Understand the trends.

- Learn how real estate works

- Run all potential scenarios.

- Risk–benefit analysis.

- Have an open mind.

Financing Real Estate Investments

Financing a real estate investment is an important topic because without real estate investment financing knowledge, investing remains a dream.

Properties and the opportunities they present revolve around financing. What kind of financing works best is a function on running and analyzing the numbers for a property. The investor's exit strategy ties in with the chosen financing.

Financing options also differ for various property types. For example, single-family home investment properties are often bought all-cash or with traditional loan product mortgages. Traditional mortgages usually require a 15-20% down payment, although subprime loans with lower down payments are back.

Essentially, those with credit scores below 680 will be in the subprime category. Those with credit scores between 680 and 739 for prime and those above that score qualify for super prime. The classifications reflect the kind of risk banks perceive through these credit scores.

The major difference between the subprime loans of 2005 through 2008 appears to be that the loans are based on the actual income of the borrower now versus allowing borrowers to state income. Several banks, including Wells Fargo and Bank of America, offer what is essentially subprime under different names. These loans allow people who have poor or no credit to qualify - and with 3% or less of the purchase price.

For a 2-4 unit building, you could qualify for owner-occupied financing with little money down (less than the usual 20%) so long as you live in one of the units.

Use as little of your own money as possible. None of your own money in the deal is preferable. The same applies to credit. The idea is to leverage by working with other people's money and credit. Here is where the right partners and mentors come into play.

Nevertheless, traditional real estate financing remains an option. But whether to use traditional financing depends in large measure on the real estate investor's income, debt, and credit score. Traditional financing requires a minimum of 10% of a down payment.

A better way to finance real estate deals is through owner-financing, also known as seller carry-back. This type of financing depends on the seller owning the property free and clear and agreeing to carry the note and receive agreed upon monthly payments.

Another option in financing investments is known as subject-to (existing financing). With subject-to financing, the real estate investor purchases the property on the condition that the existing financing stays in place. While the title is transferred, the loan remains in the seller's name, and the buyer/investor makes the payments. An investor needs no money to employ this strategy but a subject-to deal must be executed correctly to protect all parties.

The seller could also provide a second mortgage, known as seller second. Ordinarily, the seller second covers whatever the down payment is, say 20% of the purchase price. Using this method also ensures that the real estate investor uses none of his or her own money. You will, however, finance the remaining amount the traditional way and that means using your credit. And you must make sure that the loan you will get allows for a second mortgage.

Next, lease options provide a real estate buyer with the option to purchase a property. Most often the buyer pays a lump sum up front, known as the option money, then continues to pay above-market rent on the property. This is an attractive option for people with poor credit, who do not otherwise qualify for a property. The real estate investor makes money through the lease option agreement, finances any down payment he or she may have for the property with the option money yet has no landlord issues.

What to do if you live in an area with high property prices?

For real estate investors who live in places where real estate values are high, as in the San Francisco Bay Area, finding a real estate investment that provides cash flow is almost impossible, unless the investor buys all cash. But when buying all cash, there is no financial leverage in place which means that the investor's own money is tied up in the property. This situation affects the investor's return. Investors in areas with high property values bank on future appreciation versus on cash flow.

Consider that even with a loan on such a property, the investor still has to put 20 to 30% down and pay for closing costs as well as necessary repairs. In the San Francisco Bay Area that means the investor must plunk down anywhere between $200,000 and $400,000 right from the start. We are assuming an average property price of a million dollars in this illustration. Getting a high cash flow return on this investment is unlikely, especially when first owning the property.

The only way the investor sees a cash flow return is for her to buy property in a much lower priced market, a market with homes for $200,000 and below. The other possible way already mentioned is seller financing. Just know that in high property value markets, sellers display less desire to continue having a loan in place and would rather cash out of the property. Supply and demand economics help the seller accomplish this.

For real estate investors low on cash but high on desire and creativity, the possibility of buying a 2-4 unit building and then living in one of the units as an owner-occupier could work. In that scenario, the property usually needs work and the investor both lives there and repairs it. This process takes time, often a minimum of a year. Once at least a year has passed, and the property's condition has improved, the investor puts the property on the market and moves on to the next one. In theory, this sounds good and entirely feasible but one year is not a lot of time. The strategy implies that the investor will be moving many times until he or she has built up a property portfolio.

The Value of Inspections

Every home buyer and investor and their competent agent is well-served in adding a home inspection to their due diligence arsenal. It may reveal potential issues and drawbacks the home may have. Note:

a home inspection is a visual inspection. Walls etc. remain intact. But experienced inspectors' trained eyes provide insight.

In the best-case scenario, a home inspection confirms the condition of the home. It potentially provides negotiating points, or it can even pinpoint issues that are complete deal breakers.

Although home inspections are visual inspections only, think of them as insurance. They allow you to analyze the property before committing to the purchase. Home inspections can be contingencies in contracts. Even 'as-is' contracts contain them. They, therefore, offer protection for the buyer at a minimal cost, usually around $450. Sellers can benefit by providing a home inspection as part of the disclosures. Knowing the issues their home has can be invaluable. Possible negotiation points arising from an inspection might either no longer apply or be mitigated.

Consult with your real estate agent regarding the home inspections. Ask them how best to use them and where to locate qualified and excellent home inspectors. You can find them online or by word of mouth.

What Lenders Look For

The most important component in a lender's decision to tender a loan on a property is the property itself. A multi-family property speaks volumes to the lender. Its location, neighborhood, and demographics give the lender confidence or, if not, the lender eliminates it from consideration. In addition, the lender's decision derives from the property's tenant base, existing leases, turnover, and vacancy rates. Other considerations include whether the property has individual meters, its monthly operating expenses, its overall condition, its roof type and condition, and necessary capital expenses.

None of these components are about the borrower, yet they are what the lender bases his decision on to a large degree. They account for some 60 to 70% of the lender's decision to lend.

Lenders hedge their bets and evaluate the borrower as well. They will consider the borrower's credit rating, financial statements and tax returns, borrower experience, and sufficient, easily accessible borrower funds.

Knowing this means that the multi-family real estate investor can prepare all the necessary items for the lender's review. The due diligence on the property itself goes a long way here. And these components present a 'flow chart' for the way many real estate transactions are qualified and consummated.

That's the good news.

The bad news is that it is imperative to set up relationships with lenders who deal in the specific real estate niche and possibly its sub-niche ahead of time. Doing so minimizes surprises when transactions are in progress. For instance, many lenders offer loan products in the multi-family space but not all lenders lend on all multi-family properties. Make sure to know the lender's guidelines and which type of multi-family properties they will lend on. Some lenders will only lend on certain property classes, in the case of multi-family properties often only on Class A properties. If the property you have evaluated and are seeking financing for falls into Class B or C, the lender may not be able to deliver.

Unfortunately, you will have to interview lenders to find out whether they do the type of loan you seek. Make sure to know this before you find a multi-family property and definitely before you are under contract and paying for appraisals and inspection reports! It can be an expensive lesson to find out at the eleventh hour that the lender cannot do the loan you need. The scenario only allows canceling the contract.

The best thing a multi-family real estate investor can do is to find a lender who specializes in multi-family property loans. Expertise matters here because investing in multi-family properties is based on cash flow. Plus, the terms a lender who specializes in such loans vary significantly from loans banks sell to single family home consumers. Those different terms mean different monthly mortgage payments, which in turn mean different cash flow.

Sniffing Loot

A realtor and real estate investor in Indianapolis whose Christian morals drew in many investors bought many single-family homes in the area he lived and worked in. He and his then-wife sold many of these properties to other real estate investors by allowing the investors to come without having to qualify for loans on the properties. The real estate investor clients simply made the mortgage payment plus a factored in fee to the original investor. They also put down between 8-20% of the purchase price initially.

The original investor found tenants for the homes, some of whom he had simply taken over when he bought the properties. That meant he had a cash flow component already built into his offering to the investors he 'sold.' He and his team, consisting of his wife, a contractor, and a property manager milked this baby by establishing a property management company the investors had to hire on.

Although convenient, the company had accounting issues. The contractor wrote his own ticket, maintaining the properties at bare minimum, something that showed up long after owning the properties and through tenant interviews. – This property management company got horrible reviews from all the tenants in the properties.

The original realtor and investor had bought most of the properties he owned from a local bank. He and the bank manager developed a close, synergistic relationship. He purchased in bulk (the bank's tape) with the feedback and advice of the local bank's manager. The loans were as good as guaranteed. And for a long time.

Next Mr. Original Investor decided to make more money by appealing the property taxes. The assessor's office refused his request several times, but that just gave him more time to pay the taxes. It also led the municipality to figure it out. Eventually they granted him the tax reduction.

His investors believed he had as good as received the property tax reduction. They kept asking about when this property tax issue would be resolved and told that everything was in process and on track. Obviously, the investors could not approach the property tax division themselves; the property tax division cannot legally divulge such information, other than to say that property taxes are delinquent by such-and-such amount.

The investors were sold! All of them had contracts in hand that guaranteed their investment with the underlying real estate (the property). The appraisals looked good, but it later turned out they were inflated. All the investors received the monthly income from the properties. Everything seemed fine.

... Until Mr. Original Investor decided he wanted to up his game and make more money. His plan was to become a real estate developer. The properties he had 'sold' to other real estate investors served as collateral for this purpose. He ran all this through the same local lender. Unfortunately, the local bank began to scrutinize his holdings. Worse, the bank also merged with a larger bank. Discrepancies showed up. The bank investigated. It ran reports and numbers, then pulled the loans on all the properties previously funded. As for the development: not approved.

Our original investor sat in shock. He began much more regular talks with the local bank director, a kind-hearted man sitting in a morass himself. A man on his way out. The director agreed to talk to the investor's investors. He offered to 'help' them by letting them catch up on the property taxes and renegotiating the loan into their names. This scenario was a race against time.

So long as he remained director there was hope. But he was a banker, and he moved slowly. His successor had no interest in pursuing this course of action. He was instead determined to get these non-performing assets off his books - for good.

Game over. Mr. Original Investor said he cared deeply about his investors. Then he disappeared never to answer his phone or e-mail from these pesky investors who had afforded him his lifestyle again.

Understanding lenders' requirements

All lenders have specific loan products with specific requirements for underwriting the loan. Loans for single-family homes are relatively straightforward. They are based on the property the loan covers and include condition, neighborhood, market and the like. They are also based on the borrower's financials and assess his risk to the lender. Down payments for residential properties significantly vary - from 0 to 20% of the price offered for the property. Concerning down payments, the market environment will usually dictate what is acceptable. Although all numbers in a contract are negotiable, not all numbers are realistic. Lenders also have insurance requirements that must be met.

A couple qualifying for a specialty loan entered into contract for a property for which they scraped together the down payment. The property was a condo in a 2-unit building in San Francisco. The lender application was complete and all supporting documents from the realtor had arrived within a day of getting an accepted contract. Those documents included the property's insurance policy, a document lenders require. All went well until several weeks into the transaction when the lender advised that the property insurance was insufficient. Therefore, the loan could not go into the full underwriting process until the insurance had been brought up to date. The mortgage professional failed to let the parties know that the lender was unlikely to lend on this specific property for several other reasons.

That seemed easy enough, but the sellers suddenly dragged their feet and then insisted that the policy in place was not only sufficient but all that would be supplied. Intense negotiations to resolve this issue commenced. The issue would not go away. Time was running out. Because all of this happened right after all contingencies had been removed, the selling agent advised the buyers that they needed to have a backup plan, in this case another loan in place.

The buyers balked at this even though they were at high risk of breaching the contract as they were unable to procure the necessary loan. Instead of working on a backup plan, they began to blame the sellers for dragging their feet and not delivering what they needed to close. The reason for this became apparent in due time: the buyers could not find another lender to loan the amount they needed to close. They would have to come up with considerably more money to honor the contract. The original loan agent was no help to them and did not even return phone calls. In the end, the buyers lost a portion of their initial deposit, even though the seller was entitled to a full 3% liquidated damages.

Commercial real estate loans are easier to obtain than residential real estate loans because they are usually based on a property's income. Aside from the income, the commercial lender wants to know what the investor intends to do with the property as that affects income and appreciation potential down the line.

An important piece of information is exactly what kind of loans specific lenders will or won't do. Save yourself the time and headache of finding out that the lender you chose cannot lend on either the property type or its sub-class before signing a contract.

Lessons learned:

- Teamwork & communication are pivotal to all real estate transactions

- Blame does not produce positive results.

- Understand your financials, including reserves, well before writing a contract.

- Have a backup plan.

- Make sure the property you want to buy can be approved by the lender.

Commercial loan applications take time to prepare. They include data and analyses about the property, rental rolls, tax returns, borrower financials and so on. Commercial real estate investors must present a complete presentation of all these documents to the potential lender. That means everything must be prepared simultaneously.

Construction Appraisal Anyone?

In case you are considering a major renovation of or an addition to a single-family home or a multi-family property, renovation loan might be available. Using a renovation loan requires a construction appraisal, a specialized valuation service which determines a future value of the property. The real estate investor will need several items to facilitate this type of appraisal. Remember that any of the items below can vary significantly, depending on the actual materials used. The construction appraiser will request the following:

1. Blueprints with exterior dimensions

2. Your construction budget

3. Your materials list – the more detailed, the better

4. Landscaping plans.

In the best case, the appraiser understands what the property will look like after its renovation is complete.

Renovation Loans Provide Options

Renovation loans are available to buyers but they also benefit sellers. A number of renovation loans exist and Fannie Mae and the Federal Housing Administration have programs through which buyers can borrow. Through these programs, buyers can borrow based on what the property is expected to be worth after the rehab. Property sellers can refinance their existing mortgage plus the renovation costs into one loan.

For either home buyers or sellers, this means that it becomes essential to get an inspection of the home which will detail the estimated renovation costs. [Note: Home inspectors cannot provide such figures. Get this done through a renovation consultant who is also familiar with the renovation loans, their requirements, and their caps. There are specific guidelines for each one of these loan products.

What you may expect for all of them is as follows:

1. Repairs must be cosmetic in nature versus being structural.

2. An appraisal will be required

3. Cover repairs that add value to the home

If you are looking to finance or re-finance homes which need a complete renovation and/or structural repairs, you could consider the FHA 203k program. Again, caps are in place. Also, know that the FHA 203k program requires a HUD inspection.

In case of a luxury home or homes that fall within higher value ranges in need of repairs, some lenders offer Jumbo renovation loans. Because details vary and can change, seek out lenders who offer renovation loans. All real estate contracts using renovation loans ought to include the phrase: 'based on renovation financing.'

Benefits to Buyers & Sellers

Renovation loans can be excellent vehicles to sell properties which would otherwise be much more restrictive. They allow buyers to consider properties they otherwise cannot consider because they now can pay for the renovations. This is also a benefit to home sellers because the pool of buyers just increased for them and such a loan program makes their home much more marketable. That is especially true if they do not wish to do any home renovation themselves.

The home seller can also benefit by doing the renovation themselves, then selling their home for market value in real estate markets where that makes sense. The San Francisco real estate market is one such market. The same applies to the rest of the Bay Area real estate markets.

CHAPTER 4

CROWDFUNDING

Crowdfunding is all about finding investors and/or financing for a deal. In the past decade, a number of crowdfunding platforms have entered space and become one potent way to fund real estate investments. The pooling of funds allows real estate investors to get into the real estate investing game even if they have limited funds. Crowdfunding platforms usually prescribe minimum investment amounts. Many of them consider accredited investors only. Those funds allow investors to scale up and invest in much larger projects with potentially much larger returns that they could not do on their own. Many real estate developers rely on crowdfunding methods. Still, some crowdfunding platforms allow $5000 as a minimum investment.

In real estate investing access to capital is the name of the game. Crowdfunding is one way to provide such access. You might wonder where the difference between crowdfunding and real estate syndication falls. They are connected. Real estate syndication provides the structure and the plan. Crowdfunding provides the funds to execute.

Access to capital is a big deal. Without it, even the best intention to invest in real estate falls fallow. Because banks are highly regulated, access to capital is more difficult through banks. Evaluation criteria for funding through banks are stringent. Hard-money lenders tend to be local and expensive. Crowdfunding and peer-to-peer lending are alternatives. Crowdfunding platforms with 506c borrowers offer exposure to a worldwide pool of investors.

Crowdfunding is often faster and circumvents traditional financing, allows for faster closes. Credit scores are less important, and rates are comparable to those of traditional lenders. Because crowdfunding is an online medium, it allows investors and developers to take on new projects differently. They no longer need to find their target audience, present to that audience, gain its trust, etc. Instead many potential investors find them. All that besides the aim to get a large ROI without red tape and other headaches.

Crowdfunding can be applied to regular real estate purchasers (e.g. home buyers - providing purchase loans) and also can provide bridge loans, refinances, new construction and renovation loans.

Numerous crowdfunding platforms which offer anything from commercial real estate project financing to rehabs, etc. Crowdfunding is a housing market stimulus and might even contribute to stimulating affordable housing. According to Patch of Land, a crowdfunding company, ' the goal of POL's real estate crowdfunding is to solve the problem of inefficient, fragmented, and opaque real estate lending.'

Patch of Land also believes that 'crowdfunding is the perfect vehicle to introduce your brand to accredited investors around the world.' The company's stated goal includes 'rebuilding metropolitan areas, increasing property values, creating jobs, and stimulating local economies throughout the nation.' In the process of doing this, Patch of Land claims to provide investors with 12.5% average yield on investment.

Tax strategies for real estate

Real estate tax strategies are essential parts of financial planning and execution. They may also be part of the investment property exit strategy. Tax strategies and estate planning warrant consultation with estate planners and CPAs who understand real estate investing. Saving and deferring capital gains taxes is one of the major goals for efficient tax strategies. Both 1031 Exchanges and self-directed IRAs are powerful tax strategy tools for a real estate investor. While other tools exist, we will discuss only 1031 Exchanges and self-directed IRAs here. Please explore this topic further with your financial professional and via books and courses.

Self-Directed IRAs

Like many people, you are interested in maximizing your retirement investments. Most likely you recognize that money in 401(k)s is mainly in mutual funds. Other retirement accounts are generally invested in stocks, bonds, and mutual funds. You have NO control over these vehicles.

If you currently have a 401(k) plan, a regular IRA, a 403(b) plan, investigating and setting up a self-directed IRA will be worth your time. It is a tool for you to get educated about options that may be completely new to you. It is also a tool for you to gain control over your retirement investments. It is a huge step in the direction of financial freedom and living a great life in your golden years.

That may sound like a dream and a big promise. Read on for more information and join countless others on this journey.

You probably know that social security is on the brink of bankruptcy if not already bankrupt. Whether you and your children will actually see benefits that can support you even halfway is a big question mark. Most Americans no longer get pensions. Should you have a pension count your lucky stars because they are disappearing.

Counting on social security benefits promises you a small life because these benefits will be very slim or even have gone away by the time you retire. If you are close to retirement now, you will get benefits that will support you minimally. Social security was never intended to fund people's retirement yet a large percentage of people in the

United States are dependent on these disappearing benefits. The situation is really dire.

All these are important reasons to have a truly Self-Directed IRA and to control your investments through them.

Did you know that a truly self-directed IRA is blessed by the government? You and everyone in your family can and ought to benefit from this. By the way, most financial advisors say that you will need about 70% of your pre-retirement earnings to maintain your pre-retirement standard of living.

Social security retirement benefits will only replace about 40% of those. That percentage is even lower for people in the upper-income brackets. For low-income earners social security benefits are lower yet. So there is absolutely no way around it. No doubt you will have to supplement your benefits with either a pension, savings or investments.

Setting up a self-directed IRA provides many options and benefits. Under some plans, real estate investors can contribute more than $50,000 a year to their self-directed IRAs and receive the tax write-offs for those contributions.

Just what is a Self-Directed IRA?

A 401(k), 403(b) or an IRA that sits with a brokerage house such as Charles Schwab, Fidelity etc., only allows you to invest in their products. Real estate is not an investment option there.

Let me ask you this, how well are your retirement investments currently doing or do

you even know? Many people have no idea what their retirement accounts stand at, what their balances are because it is frankly too depressing to look at them. If you are averaging a 3 - 10 percent return, know that is very good for such accounts. But such returns harbor a slim chance of getting you closer to your retirement needs or goals.

In a truly self-directed IRA you have the ability to take control. You have the option of putting your money in other investments, including in real estate. And returns range anywhere from a more conservative 6-8% to 15% and up. This all depends on the assets you fund in your self-directed IRA. Note that you must do all the due diligence discussed in this book for each and every asset in your self-directed IRA.

As you now know, a truly Self-Directed IRA gives you control over your investments. And the investments are either tax-deferred or tax-free when you get your profits. That is flat out an awesome tool to grow your investments and to grow your monies. It also gives you asset protection and is important in effectively planning your estate.

Your company, bank or brokerage firm will tell you that the IRA, 401k or 403b you have through them is self-directed. What they don't tell you is that the accounts you hold through them are self-directed in so far as you invest in their products. No other investment options exist in those accounts. Many people are confused about this. This, in turn, leads many consumers to leave their accounts as is and never move on to a truly self-directed IRA.

As a shareholder or owner of stocks, bonds or mutual funds, you have little to no control over the investment. You are simply directing your money into a fund or stock or bond and the markets drive the stock including the company that the stock belongs to. Put another way while you could call up the CEO of the company whose stock you own and request the company improve its performance. The request will get no action. In stark contrast to this, real estate investing in a truly Self-Directed IRA gives you much more control over your investments.

Having the ability to control your investments absolutely cannot be underestimated. Maybe you are disenchanted with the retirement accounts that you currently have. Maybe you don't even know what they are worth or what return they are yielding. If so, read on. Isn't it time to take a look at how you may set yourself free and leave a legacy for those you love? Get the power of that yet?

Let's briefly talk about security. If you lived through the early 2000s, the Dotcom Bust, you know what can happen to stocks, bonds, and mutual funds. Of course, some do very well. What are the odds you invested in a well-performing asset?

Although all investments hold risks, it might be wise to consider investments that give you more control plus potential superior returns. Some such investments include tax liens, raw land, single-family homes, commercial properties, condos, mobile homes and so on.

Real-life examples of real estate investing in a self-directed IRA:

Land investment in a Self-Directed IRA

Long-term strategy

Find, analyze, and purchase a raw land parcel through your self-directed IRA. This is also known as land banking. Ordinarily, investing in land generates no immediate income, and the goal is to sell the land once it has appreciated. In the meantime, understand that you will have to pay property taxes and the custodian's fees for the asset through your self-directed IRA.

Note investing in a Self-Directed IRA

Long-term strategy

Find, analyze, and purchase a note secured by real estate through your self-directed IRA. Note investing generally provides you monthly income that flows back into your self-directed IRA account. Rates of return are 8-12% on average.

Rental property investing in a Self-Directed IRA

Short- or long-term strategy

Find, analyze, and purchase a rental property which can be a single-family home, a condo, a multi-family building, or an apartment building through your self-directed IRA. You cannot own your primary residence through a self-directed IRA.

Once the property is in the self-directed IRA, all rental proceeds from that property must flow into the self-directed IRA. The account pays all property expenses as well.

Let's say you purchase a single-family home for $25,000. You then improve the property by adding a bathroom or a bedroom for another $25,000. You just improved the property. Now you can charge a higher rent. That means your total cost for the property stands at $50,000, paid through your self-directed IRA.

Now you put a tenant in the property and it generates rental income of $10,000 a year. After several years of holding it, the property has appreciated considerably, and you sell it for $125,000. All of this happens inside your self-directed IRA. And you are saving the federal, state and local taxes you would need to pay when holding the property outside the self-directed IRA.

Note: although you may be able to obtain a loan to purchase property, self-directed IRA investments are generally cash transactions. Specific rules about self-directed IRA financing and tax consequences exist, so find a professional to guide you through the process and to help you avoid pitfalls and/or penalties. If you were to obtain a loan for property held in a self-directed IRA, this loan would be a non-recourse loan.

Non-recourse loans are a specialty product in the United States. In other countries, non-recourse loans are more common. In the United States, you will have to find a loan agent who specialized in non-recourse loans. These loans also have special requirements. Usually the down payment is greater and loan rates are higher. This offsets that the bank cannot go after the property if the borrower defaults. The property does not secure the loan.

The examples above only demonstrate some possible self-directed IRA investments. Others exist. Taking control of your financial future and freedom, and to live a bigger, larger life when you retire rather than living small which is what most people do.

What are your dreams? Do you want to travel, fund a foundation, educate people, or leave wealth to your heirs? It's a fantastic way to accomplish this.

Utilizing a Self-Directed IRA

How is your retirement account doing? Is it growing, flat, or losing money? Even if your company contributes dollars to your 401(k) plan, you have little to no control over that money. It is likely invested in–usually poor-performing–mutual funds. If you've ever wondered whether there is an alternative, establishing and investing through a self-directed IRA might be worth your time.

You may already have a traditional IRA or a Roth IRA through a brokerage firm such as Charles Schwab or Merrill Lynch. Those firms will tell you that these accounts are 'self-directed.' The missing piece of information is that those brokerage houses allow you to invest only in products that they sell. These generally are stocks, bonds, and mutual funds.

In contrast, a truly self-directed IRA provides you many more investment options, including real estate, private placements, and tax lien investing. These accounts must be set up with a special kind of brokerage house, such as Pencso, U-Direct, Equity Trust, Guidant Financial, and IRA Services. As of this writing, more self-directed IRA custodians are in existence than a mere decade earlier.

Growing your nest egg through this type of account with investments you have more control over, help you achieve your financial goals more easily and faster. The returns are often higher as well. Consider doing so with a Roth IRA for fantastic tax benefits as well. As a real estate investor investing and leveraging through a self-directed IRA makes good sense.

Make sure you engage the services of a knowledgeable real estate agent or mortgage professional who understands how these accounts work. These professionals can also guide you in what to do and how to present you opportunities that dovetail with your strategy of cash flow, appreciation, or both.

The 1031 Exchange

United States tax law paragraph 1031 allows real estate investors to defer capital gains taxes and to recapture taxes paid. The underlying idea of the law is to stimulate the United States economy by helping real estate investors to exchange a property for like-kind property.

Although the new tax code spells some changes for 1031 exchanges, the exchange has been preserved for those who own real property for business use and for investment purposes. The new tax code, effective 1 January 2018, disallows personal property exchanges. Its effects are yet unknown to their full extent. One of the effects the new tax code has is a $1.4467 trillion increase in the federal deficit (per the Congressional Budget Office). The full legislation effects are not yet clear. Nor is it clear where monies to cover the deficit will come from. 1031 exchanges allow real estate investors to leverage their money without having to get another loan in place.

But perhaps equally powerful about 1031 Exchanges, which apply to investment properties only, is the concept of like-kind exchange. Let's say an investor currently owns a property worth $1,000,000 in the San Francisco Bay Area. He does an exchange that replaces that property with several properties in lower property price areas or states, potentially increasing his or her cash flow immediately.

1031 Exchanges are technically complex, have strict timelines, and require expert assistance. Several types of 1031 Exchanges exist and among those the delayed like-kind exchange is the most common. In this type of exchange, the investor (exchangor) relinquishes the original property before he acquires replacement property.

Several rules govern 1031 Exchanges. The exchange must be one of like-kind property to qualify under 1031 Exchange rules.

Like-Kind Property Definition: Like-Kind property is a very broad term which means that both the original and replacement properties must be of similar nature, though they can differ in size or quality. In other words, you can't exchange farming equipment for an apartment building, because they're not the same asset. In terms of real estate, you can exchange almost any type of property, as long as it's not personal property.

Next, a 1031 exchange is only applicable for investment or business property, not personal property. In other words, you can't swap one primary residence for another.

The third condition the IRS requires is that the net market value and equity of the property purchased must be the same as, or greater than the property sold. Otherwise, you will not be able to defer 100% of the tax.

For example, if the property you are selling sells for more than the property you are exchanging under rule 1031, you are liable for the capital gains tax for the difference in those values. This difference is known as 'boot.'

This leads us to the next requirement which specifies that a taxpayer cannot receive "boot" from an exchange in order for the 1031 Exchange to be completely tax-free. If you receive boot, as in the example above, the boot is taxable for the realized gain. In other words, you can carry out a partial 1031 exchange, in which the new property is of lesser value, but this will not be 100% tax-free. This option is completely acceptable and often used when a seller wants to make some cash and is willing to pay some taxes to do so.

Also, be aware that the tax return and the name on the property title, the one being sold, must be the same as on the new property's title and tax return. However, an exception to this rule occurs in the case of a single member limited liability company (smllc), which is considered a pass-through to the member. Therefore, the smllc may sell the original property, and that sole member may purchase the new property in their individual name.

The property owner has 45 calendar days after closing on the first property to identify up to three potential properties of like-kind. – The 200% rule is the only exception. It allows the exchangor to identify four or more properties if the value of those four combined does not exceed 200% of the value of the property sold.

Finally, 1031 Exchange rules require the exchange to be complete 180 days after the sale of the exchanged property or on the due date of the income tax return (with extensions) for the tax year in which the relinquished property was sold, whichever is earlier.

Following these rules and the exact timelines specific to a 1031 Exchange require experienced parties. 1031 Exchange specialized title companies efficiently facilitate such exchanges. Investors derive great benefits from 1031 Exchanges because their money keeps working for them and they defer and/or minimize their tax liability.

An investor who owns an investment property in a high property value state could exchange the property for several other properties in lower property value states, thereby increasing his income.

1031 Exchanges are powerful tools for real estate investors.

CHAPTER 5

PASSIVE OR ACTIVE INVESTING

Active and passive real estate investing are two different approaches to real estate investing. The approaches depend on the real estate investor's goals and how much time, money, knowledge, energy, and skill the investor possesses. An investor can assess how to succeed in either passive or active real estate investing once he grasps these components and relates them to the investment vehicle he chooses.

For example, someone who wants to manage a flip actively participates, while someone in a syndication passively participates. TV shows and seminars portray real estate investing as an active endeavor because this appeals to people's imaginations about ownership. Active real estate investing demands creativity, financial savvy, knowledge, commitment, and I dare say, passion. The investor owns an asset (of whichever asset class), gets his hands dirty, and must have a willingness to learn.

However, many real estate investors really want passive income, meaning money that the asset generates versus money that requires work. What they want is less work than active real estate investing offers. That is because active real estate investing by this definition sounds almost like a job or a business - and it is. Again, assessing the risks and rewards of either, together with the investor's goals and experience level, help investors decide their direction.

Active real estate investors are not lone rangers. They form partnerships with others. In partnerships, the parties' agreement in their long-term and short-term goals is critically important. Define each partner's role clearly. Aside from partnerships, active investors build teams which can include real estate professionals, contractors, lawyers, lenders, inspectors and so forth.

Active real estate investors must decide on the short-term and long-term investment goals and build contingency plans into the overall planning. Smart passive real estate investors will do this as well.

Real estate investment strategies like flipping properties or buying, holding and renting properties demand active investor involvement. In the first scenario, organizational, financial, and sales skills apply. Other important considerations might also apply, such as how long it takes to flip a property and awareness of market direction.

In the buy, hold, and rent scenario, organizational and property management skills, not to mention maintaining the property make all the difference. You can, of course, outsource many responsibilities, although outsourcing diminishes profits. Even with outsourcing, you remain the landlord and accountable.

The good news is that passive real estate investing exists and can offer handsome returns in its own right. Passive real estate investing is less hands-on yet the investor still must have at least some market knowledge and pay attention to the details of the investment. Passive real estate investors want cash flow, and beyond that asset appreciation. Investors still must create results. They must track the investment. Define what the investor's cash flow and appreciation tolerances are.

The buy, hold and rent strategy we mentioned earlier under active real estate investing could also be a passive real estate investment. A property management company could execute all aspects for the investor, for example. While the now (more) passive real estate investor is not dealing with tenant and maintenance issues in this scenario, these outside services cost money. Once investors pay all service costs, the return on investment (ROI) might be quite different.

Let's say one investor owns multi-family property, another investor has single-family homes. With a single-family home, the investor may or may not manage the property actively. Yet, a single-family home lends itself to the active approach because single-family homes hold the risk of sitting vacant at times. In that case, the investor generates no income and has other headaches that can range from maintenance issues to vandals or squatters.

On the other hand, it makes sense to manage multi-family properties through a property management company. Because the property comprises multiple units, it can absorb the management fees and other costs and fees like accounting and marketing fees. Fees for multi-family units can offer discounts. Economies of scale often allow an investor to realize the desired return even when a unit in the property is vacant.

Or in an alternate scenario, the investor could own single-family homes or condos in a certain geographic radius. The same property management company then oversees property operations. Note that condos may have more rental restrictions. Condos also have HOA fees that the investment analysis must include as they affect investment returns.

Syndications

Of course, passive real estate investing does not end here. In recent years real estate syndications have become vehicles for passive real estate investing, in large part because property prices have shot up. Access to capital remains a barrier to entry for aspiring investors. Syndications allow individual investors to pool resources with other investors, in effect increasing the purchasing power of all individuals in the pool.

Real estate syndication has been around for decades but only recently has it become more accessible to the ordinary investor. Previously, entry to real estate syndication applied to accredited and institutional investors, individuals or entities with at least $100,000 to add to the investment pool. The old version of real estate syndication also depended on one's connections. The advent of crowd funding has brought those numbers down and made it possible to become a syndication partner with less money.

Multiple property owners or owners of a multi-family investment ought to consider joining associations for their specific property type. Local associations close to where the properties are are best. Apartment or rental associations, as well as Home Owners Associations (HOA) in buildings where investors own units, are excellent ways to stay informed. Investors can also meet other investors or landlords and locate excellent management partners there.

How syndications work

Real estate syndication business structure usually is a Limited Partnership (LP) or a Limited Liability Company (LLC). In either the managing party is a General Partner or a Manager. The Manager or General Partner manages the investments and promotes them. The LP or LLC agreement spells out the incentive, a certain profit split, they receive if the investment performs well. For this reason, the syndication's profit split structure is an important consideration. Sponsors also earn asset acquisition fees which usually range from half a percent to two percent and property management fees ranging between 2 and 9%.

Syndications vary in length, from a few months to several years. Individual investors earn a preferred return on their investment. The agreement specifies the preferred return, which ranges between 5 and 10% annually. Clearly, the more money the investor contributes to a syndication, the higher the return potential.

Finding real estate syndications is as easy as entering the term into Google but many times the best syndication opportunities arise from one's personal network. When evaluating opportunities, keep in mind how syndications work. Knowing where and in what asset class the syndication invests is just as important.

Real estate syndications are passive real estate investments and the investor considering them must conduct thorough due diligence. The syndication, not any of its investors, carries all liability. Syndication investors manage no part of the syndication, only the Sponsor does. When considering a real estate syndication investors ought to know:

- What is the structure of the syndication under the two possible SEC regulations (either 506b or Exemption 506(c))?

- What are the Sponsors qualifications and track record? Do they know the investment classes, industries, and markets the syndication holds?

- How does the syndication mitigate risk?

- What strategies exist in the syndication's plans?

- What reporting periods are in place? What reports does it provide? Look at and read the earlier reports the syndication published.

- What fees does the Sponsor charge?

- What upfront fees (closing costs, lender fees, inspection fees etc.), and management fees, are in place?

- How does the syndication structure preferred returns? Are preferred returns based on the initial investment or on the actual net cash flow the asset generates?

- Take a deep look at profit splits. Do they reflect investment length, level, risk etc.?

- Does the syndication pay dividends and if so, what affects dividend payments?

- What are the syndication's tax strategies and how does this affect the individual syndication investors?

- What rights does the investor of the syndication hold? Transferable rights, voting rights, etc?

- How does anyone become a syndication member?

- Who are the syndication team members? Inspectors, contractors, lenders, title companies, property management companies belong in this category? How were they chosen? What is their track record? Who are they?

Yes, that is work. Start with these steps, communicate with the Sponsor and with one or two syndication members.

One last word on real estate syndication: if you are an active experienced real estate investor and want to start your own real estate syndication, you can do so. Here the focus has been on real estate investing syndication as a passive investment vehicle.

Besides syndication, other passive real estate investing avenues include becoming a money partner to a person with experience in real estate investing (other than in syndication). Money partnerships require an operating agreement, and marketing and business plans. Each partner may have different skills. Agreements between the parties who brings what resources and how much of them clarify the experience. Resources can be money, time, energy, market and financial knowledge. What applies in evaluating real estate syndications also applies in partnerships that are not syndications.

Investing in a **Real Estate Investment Trust (REIT)** is yet another form of passive investing in mutual-fund-like shares of portfolios that hold real estate assets. Some REITs expose the investor to international assets. Asset classes for REITs usually are specific and REITs trade like stocks. That means that investors do not have to buy, finance and manage real property themselves and instead collect income generated from assets that the trust holds. Several different REITs are available, such as mortgage-backed and equity REITs; REITs can also be public or private. REITs must contain at least 75% real estate assets and must distribute all earnings.

You also benefit from understanding how the IRS treats real estate investors. The IRS categorizes active real estate professionals and passive real estate investors. Taxes, of course, play an important role in any real estate investor's achievement of her goals and affect profitability. Entire books cover the different categories and ways in which the IRS treats real estate investors. It is beyond the scope of this book to discuss the fine details of real estate investment taxes.

Real estate investors owe it to themselves to investigate the potential tax treatment for their assets in the due diligence list. If the IRS, for instance, decides that your real estate investing constitutes flipping, the IRS could tax your real estate assets as regular retail inventory. Ordinary income tax rates apply to this inventory.

Active or passive investing can work well for the investor, so long as the investment strategy aligns with the investor's goal. The mystique that surrounds active real estate investing does not diminish the advantages, sometimes considerable, of more passive or entirely passive real estate investing strategies.

The IRS views real estate investors in different ways. The IRS looks at how they invest, at their time commitment to the asset/investment, and at the intent to run a business operation. The four IRS categories to know about are: real estate investor, real estate dealer, real estate professionals, and real estate developer. The IRS differentiates between an investor and a dealer, and though this discussion is beyond the scope of this book, educate yourself about it. The best way to do so is engaging a capable CPA who understands real estate investing.

Tip:

Make sure to evaluate any and all potential real estate deals by thinking through the tax consequences of the investment.

Develop Your Strategy

Real estate strategy is indispensable for long-term success. A strategy exists in all cases whether consciously elected or not. Two examples follow. Both are common. In the first example, a family decides to buy a single-family house to live in with the idea of living there a minimum of 5 years. They are ready to finance the home with 20% or more of a down payment. They intend to refinance their mortgage and have a tax strategy. They also plan for maintenance, and they plan on renovating the home.

These buyers understand that markets fluctuate, and they have the resources to carry them through a possible down market. All this in place they will probably not need to sell the home if one of them loses their job or the market crashes.

A second family also wants to own a single-family home to live in, but they want to buy with little or no money down (0-5%). The neighborhood they choose has higher prices than they can afford. Their exit strategy is to sell the property, relying on appreciation. They have no other plan, should one of them lose their job or should another big negative change occur. Since they have no other financial resources, they may not survive in a down market. This thinking rests on appreciation only, and the new owners cannot get out when the market tanks.

The two examples above represent markedly different strategies. In the first example, the purchaser assessed his financial ability, matched it to a property, then considered risks and contingencies and factored them into the purchase. In the second scenario, the purchaser has done little preparation, basing his purchase on desire and hope versus actual analysis.

The discussion, of course, applies to all types of properties, not only to single-family homes but for other properties the variables may change a bit. In general, three different valuation approaches predominate cost, sales, and income. For most multi-family valuations, the income approach is the best way to go.

Let's discuss a scenario for a multi-family property to illustrate this. For this example, we'll take a look at a 10-unit apartment building. Our investor buys a 10-unit apartment building to generate long-term income streams. He understands it may take time, sometimes years, to accomplish the goal. The investor considers all available data, such as operating expenses, tenant profile, and length of tenancies, capital expenditures, and the classification of the property (A-D). He gets professional property inspections and analyzes the seller's tax returns and any tenant leases.

In addition, he identifies ways to improve the property's net operating income and understands tax benefits. He has access to financing to buy and improve the property. He has an excellent team.

In contrast, the second investor also buys a 10-unit apartment building to collect rents from current tenant base but has no intent to improve the building. He reads the disclosures and available reports without the ability or interest to interpret them. He may also simply takes the real estate agent's or the seller's word at face value. He does not bother to verify the information or to conduct his own inspections. Although he has access to financing, he may have few resources to maintain the property and to address unforeseen necessary repairs. Next, he has not vetted his team. This investor is poorly prepared, has unrealistic expectations, and has done superficial due diligence.

Success for investor number one is much more likely even though investor number two could succeed as well. The strategy in the first scenario lays a better foundation. The second scenario counts on luck. Results for these different approaches to investing in multi-family property can vary dramatically. A larger vision and creative problem-solving to increase the net operating income for the property can reward the multi-family real estate investor.

For example, an investor who buys a property with vacant units in it could aim to remodel the apartments. Once he remodels the vacant units and rents them, he remodels other apartments as they become vacant. Done correctly, the improved property can increase the tenant profile of the building and substantially increase income. Note that improvements need to align with the building and its neighborhood. One big mistake investors make is to over-improve a property, which means the property offers upgrades, amenities and details beyond those of others in its neighborhood.

Multi-family properties in San Francisco are expensive. Many of these properties fall under rent control and assessment in that light. The tenant mix, where the building is located, what deferred maintenance it needs, whether it is on the City's Mandatory Soft Story Program list etc. differentiate these properties. If investing in multi-family buildings understand local rules, regulations, and laws. San Francisco offers low cap rates, usually between 4 to 6 percent but sometimes lower. Such rules apply in many other markets. Real estate investors must know the rules, regulations, and laws. Otherwise, they may be in for rude awakenings.

The advantage of multi-family is that everyone needs a home. Multi-family investments are also easier to understand and acquire. In contrast, retail or office buildings and leases require additional knowledge and steps. Every single number requires more specific knowledge. Single-family homes are easiest to invest in because the level of knowledge required is less than what is necessary for multi-family investing. And multi-family investing takes less knowledge than other commercial asset classes, such as office and retail buildings and warehouses.

Finally, a word about opinions of various asset classes as portrayed in the media and by the so-called experts. The wealth of opinions and information about real estate investing asset classes is stunning. In many cases, expert opinions stem from having invested in one specific asset class versus another. So long as investors recognize the bias and evaluate assets classes themselves, some of these opinions will serve them well. Indeed, they may guide investors to their interests and particular abilities.

Now back to the discussion about choosing a strategy. In strategy, less is often more because less tends to provide laser focus. Considering the different aspects, activities, and possibilities real estate investor's face, strategic planning makes a huge difference. Strategic planning combines active as well as proactive consideration of the investor's goals. It sets a framework which allows the investor to stay on track. With it, the real estate investor establishes structure, priorities, the ability to identify problems and opportunities faster and more effectively, and even helps in the clarity of communications. Just remember that plans are less important than planning and more importantly matching the real estate asset class you choose with its complementary strategy. Imagine the excitement the smorgasbord of real estate opportunities conjures up. Palpable, it creates the itch to make a move now for whatever presents itself for fear of losing out.

The flip side to planning can paralyze investors. They suddenly realize all they need to learn. The best way to learn anything remains to do it. Real estate investors are no exception though the stakes are a bit higher because the sums of money invested are higher than with other investments. Preparation and execution go hand in hand.

What is your Exit Strategy?

You have an exit strategy, right?

As a serious real estate investor, you have a plan, know your target market, know the numbers, and have an exit strategy. All those components announce to the world that you are a real estate professional versus a hobbyist. They set you apart from the competition. Let's look at the exit strategy.

An exit strategy is a plan specifying an investment exit. An exit strategy is a contingency plan. - While there are some people who consider appreciation a plan for their investments, counting on appreciation is a risky strategy and could even be considered speculation.

Remember that many people who bought property in the boom years in the mid-2010s have lost and are still losing money. And some are losing properties to foreclosure. Unfortunately, that includes real estate investors.

Exit strategies are ways to mitigate risk considerably and it is prudent to have at least a couple of exit strategies in place for a real estate investment. Doing so allows for flexibility in different market environments while still generating a profit.

Such strategies include wholesaling, seller finance, lease options, renting and holding, refinancing, selling the note, rehabbing, flipping, and many more.

There are money and profit in all these strategies and employing one or several of them depends on your goals, your focus, and your plan. Just know that while rehabbing properties can be quite profitable, they are potential headaches. Make sure your comfort level is on par with the strategy you employ.

Having several exit strategies is a must in real estate investing because there are things that can go wrong. These include tenant issues, the inability to secure appropriate financing, market demand issues, a buyer or lender back out, unexpected costs, declining real estate market conditions, and others.

Other Important Considerations

Becoming and being a real estate investor can be fun and very lucrative once we get past the myth that real estate investing is easy money. If you are in real estate investing to get rich quick, it is unlikely to happen. As in all businesses, the fundamentals count. And the importance of running the enterprise as a business is equally important.

Running a business requires a set of skills unfamiliar to most people. Investors must acquire them. The same applies to the right mindset. Acquiring either can be a gargantuan venture and many folks start out with a do-it-yourself approach and wasting time and money. Learning from those who are successful already will provide a huge advantage and a head start in most cases, instead of making costly mistakes.

That said, there are other important considerations for real estate investors. They are in no particular order in this article and eventually must be incorporated into a real estate investment business.

Establishing a buyer's list as well as establishing a seller's list are essential because, without either, there is no business, nor any profit. Such lists can be generated in many ways, including through posting ads on Craigslist and Yelp, blogging, social networking via Facebook, Twitter, etc., professional networking via LinkedIn, establishing websites for buyers and sellers, and through affiliate marketing.

There are many more, naturally. Get creative yet stay on target. Distractions are plentiful. Maybe experiment with one or two suggestions. But keep track of everything and implement a system. That could be a simple spreadsheet or your own handwritten notes. If writing notes by hand, make sure they are thorough and decipherable. Keep it simple initially, then eventually automate the system. You will be able to plan, focus, and execute better, and improve your real estate investment business' bottom line.

About Resources

One of the biggest obstacles many real estate investors face is that of having the resources they need at their fingertips when they need them. Most real estate investors immediately think about money when the word resources is mentioned. Other resources are time, energy, team, knowledge, experience, attitude, and mindset. Many real estate investors have an abundance of one resource and lack the others, though they are just as essential as the one they already have.

Resourcefulness, the ability to do the best with what they have and build from there, is almost always the best way to overcome obstacles. Frankly, wishing for something you don't have or blaming lack of resources for taking no action in the direction you want to move in is self-defeating. Understanding which resources you need to succeed and then taking the necessary steps to get them, on the other hand, accelerates the journey, self-confidence and success.

One mistake many real estate investors make is to take steps out of their league. For instance, I have been approached countless times by newbie investors to 'bring them deals.' The approach comes with the vague promise that they will do business with me when and if I deliver. Deliver what? Most of these folks had no idea what they were looking at nor understood much about the market. Additionally, they had done little to no homework on the financial aspects of real estate. All this amounted to the real estate investor wanting someone else, in this case, me, to do the work.

Don't be this kind of investor. Instead, understand the market and that realtors usually have access to properties listed on the market versus having secret property deals sitting around. This will save you a lot of time, render your conversation more intelligent, and actively involve you in the deal. Take small, intelligent, consistent steps toward your goal. And take them regularly.

Keep asking yourself how to bridge the gap between the resources you have and the resources you need. You might do this by articulating your vision to another party and inspire them to contribute resources they have. Obviously partnering is a whole other ball of wax, one that requires careful consideration, trust, mutual respect, and benefits for all parties involved.

SUMMING IT ALL UP

LESSONS LEARNED

- Preparation is a gem.

- Execution is an applied strategy.

- Build teams.

- Make your money when you buy.

- Treat others the way you want to be treated.

- Take your time & do it right.

- Trust and verify.

- Become a master communicator.

- Innovate.

- Understand people and communities are behind all numbers.

- Finish what you start.

- Have an apprentice mindset

- Everything pales compared to experience.

Enjoy!

Believe nothing because a wise man said it,

Believe nothing because it is generally held.

Believe nothing because it is written.

Believe nothing because it is said to be divine.

Believe nothing because someone else said it.

But believe only what you yourself judge to be true.

-Buddha

SELECTED BIBLIOGRAPHY

Many books about real estate investing exist. Not all are listed here.

Abate, G., & Losa, G. (2016). *Real Estate in Italy: Markets, Investment Vehicles and Performance* (1 edition). London ; New York: Routledge.

Bagli, C. V. (2014). *Other People's Money: Inside the Housing Crisis and the Demise of the Greatest Real Estate Deal Ever Made* (Reprint edition). New York: Plume.

Bakerson, J. R. (2013). *How to Buy Property Overseas For Profit and Lifestyle*. RevealRealEstate.com.

Berges, S. (2004a). *The Complete Guide to Buying and Selling Apartment Buildings* (2 edition). Hoboken, N.J: Wiley.

Berges, S. (2004b). *The Complete Guide to Real Estate Finance for Investment Properties: How to Analyze Any Single-Family, Multifamily, or Commercial Property* (1 edition). Hoboken, N.J: Wiley.

Blinder, A. S. (2013). *After the Music Stopped: The Financial Crisis, the Response, and the Work Ahead* (Reprint edition). New York, NY: Penguin Books.

Briggman, S., & Therriault, K. (2016). *Real Estate Crowdfunding Explained: How to get in on the explosive growth of the real estate crowdfunding industry*. CreateSpace Independent Publishing Platform.

Bronchick, W., & Licata, G. (2007). *Defensive Real Estate Investing: 10 Principles for Succeeding Whether Your Market is Up or Down* (Original edition). New York: Kaplan Publishing.

Brown, P. H. (2018). *How Real Estate Developers Think: Design, Profits, and Community* (Reprint edition). University of Pennsylvania Press.

Brown, T. H. (2013). *How Money Walks - How $2 Trillion Moved Between the States, and Why It Matters* (2 edition). Worzalla.

Brueggeman, W. B., & Professor, J. F. (2015). *Real Estate Finance & Investments* (15 edition). New York, NY: McGraw-Hill Education.

Cao, J. A. (2015). *The Chinese Real Estate Market: Development, Regulation and Investment* (1 edition). Abingdon, Oxon ; New York, NY: Routledge.

Collins, N., & Collins, A. (2018). *The Savvy Seller: Use Seller Financing to Sell Your Property for Top Dollar and Receive Income for Life* (1 edition). CreateSpace Independent Publishing Platform.

Crook, D. (2006). *The Wall Street Journal. Complete Real-Estate Investing Guidebook.* New York: Crown Business.

Dorkin, J., & Turner, B. (2013). *BiggerPockets Presents: The Ultimate Beginner's Guide to Real Estate Investing.* BiggerPockets Publishing, LLC.

Durrett, C., Thomas, W. H., & Adams, P. (2009). *The Senior Cohousing Handbook: A Community Approach to Independent Living, 2nd Edition* (2nd edition). New York: New Society Publishers.

Eastman, P. (2013). *Building Type Basics for Senior Living* (2 edition). Hoboken: Wiley.

Farmer, E. B. (2017). *The Land Flipper on Owner Financing: How To Use Seller Financing to Accrue Real Estate Notes and Generate Passive Income.* CreateSpace Independent Publishing Platform.

Fernandez, E. (2016). *1031 Exchanges Made Easy.* CreateSpace Independent Publishing Platform.

Gallinelli, F. (2015). *What Every Real Estate Investor Needs to Know About Cash Flow... And 36 Other Key Financial Measures, Updated Edition* (3 edition). New York: McGraw-Hill Education.

Gerdes, L. I. (2014). *The American Housing Crisis* (annotated edition). Farmington Hills, Michigan: Greenhaven Press.

Gordon, P. (1998). *Seniors' Housing and Care Facilities: Development, Business, and Operations* (3 edition). Washington, D.C: Urban Land Institute.

Greene, D. (2017). *Long-Distance Real Estate Investing: How to Buy, Rehab, and Manage Out-of-State Rental Properties.* BiggerPockets.

Hennessey, B. (2015b). *The Due Diligence Handbook For Commercial Real Estate: A Proven System To Save Time, Money, Headaches And Create Value When Buying Commercial Real Estate* (Second edition). United States: CreateSpace Independent Publishing Platform.

Horn, J. S. (n.d.). *The ABC's of 1031 Exchanges and Triple Net Lease Properties.*

Keller, G., Jenks, D., & Papasan, J. (2005). *The Millionaire Real Estate Investor* (1 edition). New York: McGraw-Hill Education.

Kennedy, J. F., Smith, M., & Wanek, C. (Eds.). (2001). *The Art of Natural Building: Design, Construction, Resources.* Gabriola Island, BC: New Society Publishers.

Lake, L. J. (2015). *Seller Financing: Real Estate Investing for Anyone.* Vassar International Publishing.

Lantrip, M. (2017). *How To Do A Section 1031 Like Kind Exchange: Simultaneous, Delayed, Reverse, Construction* (1.0 edition). Anderson Logan, LLC.

Lindahl, D. (2008). *Multi-Family Millions: How Anyone Can Reposition Apartments for Big Profits* (1 edition). Hoboken, N.J: Wiley.

Linneman, P. (2016). *Real Estate Finance and Investments Risks and Opportunities, Fourth Edition* (4th edition). Linneman Associates.

Long, C. (2011). *Finance for Real Estate Development.* Washington, DC: Urban Land Institute.

Manganelli, B. (2014). *Real Estate Investing: Market Analysis, Valuation Techniques, and Risk Management* (2015 edition). New York: Springer.

Marcuse, P., & Madden, D. (2016). *In Defense of Housing: The Politics of Crisis.* London ; New York: Verso.

McElroy, K. (2012b). *The ABCs of Real Estate Investing: The Secrets of Finding Hidden Profits Most Investors Miss* (Reprint edition). Minden, NV: RDA Press, LLC.

McNellis, J. (2016). *Making It in Real Estate: Starting Out as a Developer* (None edition). Urban Land Institute.

Murray, B. H. (2017b). *Crushing It in Apartments and Commercial Real Estate: How a Small Investor Can Make It Big* (1 edition). Sackets Harbor Press.

Murray, C., Monetti, E., & Ween, C. (2017). *Real Estate and Urban Development in South America: Understanding Local Regulations and Investment Methods in a Highly Urbanised Continent* (1 edition). Abingdon, Oxon ; New York, NY: Routledge.

Owusu-Ansah, A. (2018). *Construction and Application of Property Price Indices* (1 edition). Abingdon, Oxon ; New York, NY: Routledge.

Pearce, B. W. (2007). *Senior Living Communities: Operations Management and Marketing for Assisted Living, Congregate, and Continuing Care Retirement Communities* (2nd edition). Baltimore: Johns Hopkins University Press.

Poorvu, W. J., & Cruikshank, J. L. (1999a). *The Real Estate Game: The Intelligent Guide To Decisionmaking And Investment*. New York, NY: Free Press.

Roberts, R. R., & Cummings, C. (2009). *Financing Real Estate Investments For Dummies* (1 edition). Hoboken, NJ: For Dummies.

Rosen, K. D. (2017). *Investing in Income Properties: The Big Six Formula for Achieving Wealth in Real Estate* (2 edition). Hoboken: Wiley.

Schaeffer, J. (2014). *Real Goods Solar Living Sourcebook: Your Complete Guide to Living beyond the Grid with Renewable Energy Technologies and Sustainable Living* (14th edition). Gabriola Island, BC, Canada: New Society Publishers.

Schaub, J. (2016). *Building Wealth One House at a Time, Updated and Expanded, Second Edition* (2 edition). New York: McGraw-Hill Education.

Sharkey, B. B. (2017). *Senior Housing.* CreateSpace Independent Publishing Platform.

Sivori, R. J., & P, F. (2017). *Creative Real Estate Financing: Seller / Buyer Win! Win!* (1 edition). CreateSpace Independent Publishing Platform.

Stegmaier, J. (2015). *A Crowdfunder's Strategy Guide: Build a Better Business by Building Community* (1 edition). Oakland: Berrett-Koehler Publishers.

Stein, M., & Lewis, T. (2015). *Seller Financing and Real Estate Notes in the Dodd-Frank Era: by Seller Finance Consultants Inc.* Seller Finance Consultants Inc.

Sutherland, C. (2015). *Creative Real Estate Seller Financing: How to Use Seller Financing to Buy or Sell Any Real Estate.* CES Sutherland Management LLC.

Sutton, G. (2013). *Loopholes of Real Estate.* Scottsdale, AZ: RDA Press, LLC.

Turner, B. (2015). *The Book on Rental Property Investing: How to Create Wealth and Passive Income Through Intelligent Buy & Hold Real Estate Investing!* (1 edition). Denver: BiggerPockets.

Woolley, T., & Porritt, J. (2006). *Natural Building: A Guide to Materials and Techniques.* Ramsbury: Crowood Press.

APPENDIX A – RESOURCES

Many more resources than the ones listed below exist.

International Bitcoin Real Estate Association

https://www.ibrea.network/

Patch of Land

www.patchofland.com

Commercial real estate crowdfunding platform

www.crowdstreet.com

Realty Shares (accredited investors only)

www.realtyshares.com

Global real estate listings

www.leadingre.org

Real estate data sites (includes comparables)

www.propertyshark.com

www.mashvisor.com

Foreclosure site

www.bankownedproperties.org

Renovation loans

www.203konline.com

Real estate investing clubs Find via Google and MeetUp.

Real estate investing social network

www.biggerpockets.com

GLOSSARY

Agency: Relationship created via a contract or law where one party acts on behalf of another party. The relationship is fiduciary in nature.

Apartments: (see Multi-Family)

Appraisal: A property value estimate or opinion report by a licensed appraiser.

Appreciation: Increase of an asset's value.

As-is condition: Contract clause which means the property is sold in its current condition without warranties. The seller will not pay for any repairs.

Asset: Piece of property or resource with economic value.

Assignment: Transfer of ownership or of rights, liabilities, etc. via a contract.

Bridge financing (gap financing): Short-term loan in place until longer term financing takes its place.

Broker Price Opinion (BPO): A written value opinion of a property done by a licensed professional (broker).

Capitalization Rate (CAP Rate): Equals net operating income divided by sales price. Used to assess potential rate of return of a real estate investment.

Cash flow: Net amount an entity receives and disburses during an accounting period.

CC&Rs: Covenants, Conditions and Restrictions. A legal document controlling the use, restrictions, and requirements of a property.

Closing Costs: Fees that apply to finalizing a loan on a property, e.g. appraisal, title insurance, document, loan origination fees etc.

Contingency: Condition that must be met before a contract becomes binding.

Conversions – A process that changes property into a different property class as from single-family homes to multi-family units.

Credit: Ability of a consumer to obtain goods or services before payment. Based on trust that future payments will be made – assessed through credit scores.

Commercial real estate offers investors many niche markets, such as large apartment buildings (6+ units), office buildings, industrial condos and buildings, hotels, and retail buildings. Huge variety exists within each category.

Comparables (Comps) : Recently sold or listed properties with similar characteristics and in similar locations to the property you are analyzing.

Condo: Specific unit in a building to which their owner or owners receive title and ownership rights. May have residential, commercial, or industrial zoning.

Contract: A legally binding agreement between parties.

Cooperative: Form of multiple ownership in which a corporation or business trust entity holds title to a property and grants occupancy rights to shareholders.

Damages: An award paid to a party as compensation for loss or injury.

Deed: A written instrument by which title to land is transferred.

Development is the generic term for anything from re-zoning to building new buildings of all types (e.g. condos, apartments, retail, office, mixed-use, and the list goes on).

Disclosure: Statement of known facts.

Earnest money (consideration): Good-faith deposit made by a prospective property buyer. Communicates intent to complete the transaction.

Equity: The amount of interest or value a property owner holds in a property.

Escrow: Procedure in which a third party facilitates buyer's and seller's instructions and handles paperwork and distributes funds.

Eviction: Legal process of removing a tenant because of breaching the lease.

Fee Simple: An estate in which the owner has unrestricted power to dispose of property as he wishes. Represents greatest interest a person can have in real estate.

Fiduciary: Persons or entity entrusted with power or property to benefit another party.

ForeclosurevAct of taking possession of a property on which a mortgagee has defaulted.

Fraud: Crime using dishonest methods to take items of value from another.

Gross Rent Multiplier: Ratio of the price of an investment property to its annual gross rental income.

Home Owner's Association (HOA): Non-profit member association in line with a property's CC&Rs.

Land trust: Legal agreement in which a property ownner transfers the property to a trustee via a trust agreement.

Lease: Agreement transferring the right of possession of real estate for a specific period of time.

Lease option: Lease clause conveying the right to purchase a property under certain conditions.

Leverage: The ability to generate a larger rate of return with little of one's own money and through borrowed funds instead.

Liquidated Damages: A predetermined amount or percentage an injured party receives if the other party breaches the contract.

Lis Pendens: Recorded legal document that provides notice that a legal action has been filed against a property

Market Value: Value that represents the most probable price for a property in a competitive and open market.

Mobile Homes: Prefabricated housing unit attached to land semipermanently.

Modular homes/tiny homes: Prefabricated housing, often considered personal property.

Multi-Family are residential rental properties where the actual apartment building size can vary considerably. Location, apartment building size, layouts, amenities, and age break down into further classifications.

Multiple Listing Service (MLS) : Services real estate brokers offer to disseminate property information and establish contractual compensation offers for other brokers.

Negotiation: Process of reaching an agreement. The act of bargaining.

Net worth: The amount calculated from subtracting liabilities from assets.

NNN Lease: (triple net lease)Lease in which the tenant pays rent and all operating expenses.

Non-recourse loan: Loan in which the lender can pursue the property the loan is for only, and cannot go after other assets of the borrower.

Note: A debt instrument (promissory note, mortgage note)

Planned Unit Development refers to a zoning designation for residential, commercial, or industrial property developed at the same or slightly greater overall density than conventional development.

Probate: Process establishing the validity of a will and then administering it.

Prop 13 (California) : Amendment adopted in June 1978 which reduced property tax rates and restricted annual increases of assessed value.

Property Management: Maintains real property and manages aspects such as leasing, marketing, and bookkeeping.

Reciprocity: Practice or behavior for mutual benefit.

Recourse loan: A loan which allows the lender to pursue other borrower assets in addition to the loan collateral.

REITs represent more passive forms of real estate investing. Investors buy into a publicly or privately traded fund by purchasing shares of the fund. REITs usually pay a yield (%) which comes from the cash flow of the REITs underlying real estate holdings.

Rent control: Local or state government regulations which stipulate amounts of rent landlords can charge their tenants.

REO (see Foreclosure)

RESPA (Real Estate Settlement Procedures Act) Federal statute aiming to regulate informing consumers about mortgage settlement costs.

Risk of loss: Contractual terms used to determine which party is responsible for damage after the sale but before delivery.

Rule of 72 Shows the number of years to double one's money by dividing 72 by the rate of return.

Seller financing: A loan provided by the seller.

Short sale: Occurs when a property's sale will net less than amounts owed to the lender.

Single-Family Homes comprise either attached or detached homes, generally built for families and usually one- or two-story homes.

Subdivision: Tract, lot, or parcel division into more sites for the purpose of development or sale.

'Subject to': Contract clause which specifies a special condition or contingency that applies to the sale.

Syndications are legal private or public partnerships that allow investors to purchase an investment property that ordinarily would be beyond their financial means. Often structured as LLCs or LPs.

Investors generally have no management responsibilities or voting powers and are not personally liable for the syndication's actions.

Tax Deeds: Instrument that conveys legal title to a property and which is sold by a government agency for delinquent property taxes.

Tax Liens: Lien issued against a property for delinquent taxes.

Tenancy in Common (TIC) : Joint ownership of property by two or more persons. No right of survivorship.

Title: Document that provides evidence of a person's interest or right in a property.

Turnkey: A product or property ready for immediate use.

Underwriting: Lender analysis of the assumed risk in connection to a loan.

Unimproved property: Land without buildings or other improvements

Vacancy factor: Estimated vacancy allowance.

Variance: Zoning deviation request to zoning authorities which can grant it.

Zoning Regulation of structures and uses in particular zones or districts.

ABOUT THE AUTHOR

Gabrielle Dahms has been a San Francisco/Bay Area realtor for 17 years, a successful real estate investor for 10 years, and an avid yogini for 30 years. She and her toilet-trained cat live in San Francisco.

Index

With so much to consider in real estate investing, always remember the investing pitfalls of inexperience, undercapitalization, ignoring changes, and having a big ego. This book aims to make you aware of them and to provide you the resources to avoid them.

If you enjoyed this book, please watch for its sequel which addresses how to find the right markets to invest in, where to find deals, and more. Send an e-mail to REIPrimers@gmail.com so I can let you know when the next title hits the market.

Made in the USA
Monee, IL
22 March 2021